KUWAIT

BY DEBRA A. MILLER

LUCENT BOOKS
An imprint of Thomson Gale, a part of The Thomson Corporation

THOMSON
™
GALE

Detroit • New York • San Francisco • San Diego • New Haven, Conn. • Waterville, Maine • London • Munich

THOMSON

—————✦————— ™

GALE

On cover: Kuwait City, Kuwait

LIBRARY OF CONGRESS CATALOGING-IN-PUBLICATION DATA

Miller, Debra A.
    Kuwait / by Debra A. Miller.
        p. cm. — (Modern nations of the world)
Summary: Discusses the geography, history, people, and culture of Kuwait as well as the country's current challenges.
    Includes bibliographical references and index.
    ISBN 1-59018-624-9 (hard cover : alk. paper)
    1. Kuwait—Juvenile literature. I. Title. II. Series.
DS247.K8M555 2004
953.67—dc22

2004010841

Printed in the United States of America

CONTENTS

Introduction

Transformed by Oil

Most Americans knew little about the Middle East country of Kuwait until August 2, 1990, when Iraqi troops invaded and occupied it—an action that provoked the Gulf War of 1991, a United Nations military intervention led by the United States. The U.S.-led war against Iraq focused attention on Kuwait and ultimately liberated it from Iraqi control, but not before the Iraqis had inflicted significant physical and environmental damage to the country and terrorized the Kuwaiti people. The war highlighted the vulnerability of Kuwait, a tiny oil-producing country located in a volatile part of the world with no real military ability to protect itself from foreign attack.

As a result of this vulnerability, Kuwait has formed a close relationship with the United States, which offers protection and defense, as it did during the Gulf War. In exchange, the United States and other countries are assured access to Kuwait's tremendous supplies of oil and natural gas. Today, Kuwait sits on more than 9 percent of the earth's oil reserves, making it one of the richest countries in the world. The country's oil wealth has given Kuwait's rulers (called emirs) the ability to modernize the country and lift its people from poverty and illiteracy. As a result, Kuwaiti citizens today have one of the world's highest per capita (average per person) incomes; pay no taxes and are guaranteed jobs; receive generous education, health, and welfare benefits from the government; and have access to all the goods and amenities that Americans enjoy.

However, modern Kuwait reflects the legacy of its pre-oil culture. Before the discovery of oil, Kuwait was a small sheikdom, inhabited by descendants of Arab nomads who followed the Islam religion and ruled by one family, the al-Sabah. Its people struggled to survive as nomadic herdsmen, boatbuilders, and divers for pearls, once the country's most important resource. Kuwaitis also became adept at trading and seafaring, due largely to Kuwait's strategic location on the Persian Gulf and its natural, protected harbor. The Sabah family still rules Kuwait, and Islam remains the official, dominant religion.

Historian Anh Nga Longva has noted, "With the advent of oil production and the end of sea trade, Kuwait definitely turned its back on its . . . past."[1] This assertion is only partly true. The oil wealth did give Kuwaitis access to the rest of the world—access that brought materialism and an interest in consumer goods from the West along with Western dress, attitudes, and values. But these new values conflicted with the conservative values of Islam and Kuwait's traditional culture. Women and young people, in particular, challenged the traditional dress, customs, and attitudes that still prevail in some quarters. As a result, Kuwait today is a mix of traditional/Islamic culture and Western ideas. It is a place where

A young boy walks proudly with the flag of Kuwait, a tiny oil-producing country in the Middle East.

The number of modern high-rise buildings in the skyline of Kuwait City, the nation's capital, reflects the opulence of Kuwaiti society.

both traditional and Western clothing is worn, where a legislature is democratically elected but can be disbanded by the ruling emir, where nightlife and restaurants abound but alcohol is illegal, and where women hold important jobs but are not allowed to vote.

Kuwait's oil transformation changed its society in other ways. With a small native population, Kuwait relied on a large number of foreign workers to grow its economy. By the 1990s, this foreign population outnumbered Kuwaitis. Because the government limited most benefits to Kuwaiti citizens and discriminated against foreigners in other ways as well, deep class divisions emerged in Kuwait's society. These rifts created tension and instability and still pose a major problem for the country.

Kuwait's challenge, therefore, is to navigate a future that will bring together these contradictory social and religious forces. As a small, militarily vulnerable country, Kuwait also requires continued alliance with Western nations, particularly the United States, to secure its borders, while it attempts to limit Western influences. Finally, Kuwait must prepare its citizens and its economy for that day in the distant future when its life-sustaining oil runs out.

Desert by the Sea

Kuwait is a small triangle of land bordering the Persian Gulf, sandwiched between and dwarfed by two of the Middle East's major powers: Iraq and Saudi Arabia. It is one of the world's smallest countries, its entire territory slightly smaller than the state of New Jersey. Indeed, it covers an area only about 100 miles from east to west and 125 miles north to south. Most of its land is arid desert, and its population numbers only about 2 million. However, despite its small size, dry climate, and limited population, Kuwait is an important country because it is situated on top of one of the world's biggest petroleum reserves. With this fortunate location, Kuwait has become a major producer and supplier of oil and one of the Middle East's most developed and progressive countries.

Land of Sand

Kuwait's main territory comprises a roughly triangular desert area of about 6,880 square miles in the northeastern part of the Persian Gulf region (also called the Arabian Gulf). To the east, Kuwait borders the warm and beautiful waters of the Gulf. On the southern side of the triangle is Saudi Arabia, a country with whom Kuwait has developed peaceful relations. To the north and west, however, lies Iraq, a neighbor that has historically disputed its 150-mile border with Kuwait and has claimed control at various times over Kuwait's lands.

The topography of Kuwait is remarkably uniform—a flat layer of sand with no mountains, rivers, lakes, or streams. Its highest elevation is only about 1,000 feet above sea level; most of the country is below 660 feet, gradually tapering down to sea level. Along the coast of the Gulf, however, a seventeen-mile-long ridge called the Jal az-Zor rises up, forming a wall around Kuwait Bay, a natural protected harbor in the Gulf. The Jal az-Zor ridge is one of only a few areas in Kuwait that provide pastures for grazing animals; when rain falls on these hills in winter and early spring, for a short time its valleys become green fields full of grasses and other plants. A few other small ridges and hills dot the desert landscape, and cliffs, sand dunes, and saltwater marshes can be found along the coast.

There is geological evidence that Kuwait's landscape was formed thousands of years ago during the Ice Age, when streams flowed across the area to form a broad, shallow channel that today is a wide, flat desert valley on Kuwait's western side. Most of this flat desert is covered with sand and coarse gravel. Winds from the northwest often blow this sand and dust from one area to another, forming dunes of various shapes and sizes. This desert land does not support agriculture; less than 1 percent of Kuwait's land is suitable for cultivation. The poor soil, combined with scant rainfall and little water for irrigation, has meant that much of Kuwait's food

A lone camel stands in the Kuwaiti desert. Most of the country's topography is comprised of flat, arid desert with no mountains, rivers, or streams.

must be imported. Some farming is possible in areas near Kuwait's few underground reservoirs; in these areas crops such as tomatoes, melons, dates, and cucumbers are grown. In addition, there are a few successful dairy and poultry farms.

OCEAN AND ISLANDS

Because of the harshness of its desert territory, as historian Jill Crystal explains, "Kuwaitis have had to look outward, to . . . the sea."[2] Indeed, the waters of the Persian Gulf are a huge asset, providing cooling winds and recreation as well as food, trade, and commerce to Kuwait. The 181-mile-long coastline can be divided into two parts—the southern coast, which features beautiful sandy beaches, and the northern coast, which is bordered by extensive mudflats and is undeveloped in places. However, even in areas containing mudflats, such as around the capital of Kuwait City, beautiful, man-made sandy beaches and green resort areas contrast nicely with the turquoise blue Gulf waters and provide welcome relief from the hot and dry climate. Private villas and chalets are located on many of the beaches, about 11 percent of which are used for tourist recreation and entertainment.

Kuwaiti farmworkers harvest tomatoes. Despite Kuwait's scant rainfall, the country's few underground reservoirs make cultivation of certain products possible.

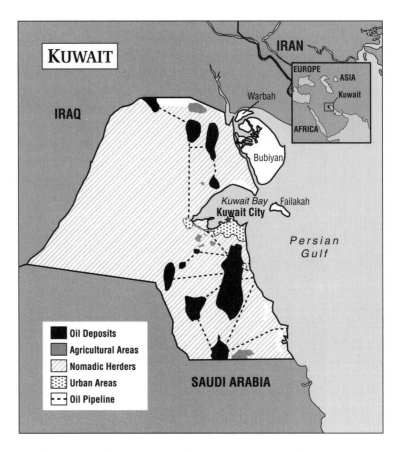

The country's most prominent water feature is Kuwait Bay, a twenty-five-mile indentation in the country's shoreline that provides an excellent natural harbor for ships. The bay makes up about half of Kuwait's Gulf coast. This asset allowed the capital city, Kuwait (unofficially called Kuwait City), to develop first as a fishing village and later as a major port and boatbuilding center. Today the port provides Kuwait with an easy way to ship its oil products abroad. In addition to Kuwait City there are six other seaports, located at Shuwaikh, Doha, Ahmadi, Mina Abdallah, Shuaiba, and Al-Zor.

Off the coast within Kuwait's twelve-mile territorial waters are nine islands—Warbah, Bubiyan, Miskan, Failaka, Auhha, Umm Al-Naml, Kubbar, Qaruh, and Umm Al-Maradim. The islands are important because they form a chain along Kuwait's coastline from north to south that provides the country with a defensive barrier on its eastern Gulf border. The largest island, north of Kuwait Bay is Bubiyan, linked to the mainland by a concrete bridge. Measuring approximately 330 square miles, the island was formed by deposits of sediment brought to the Gulf by floodwaters of the Tigris and Euphrates rivers. As a result it is very flat and muddy, and there is little vegetation other than what grows on a few sand dunes. Bubiyan and another similar but smaller island to the north, Warbah, form a natural barrier between Kuwait City and the countries of Iraq and Iran, which lie to the north and east of the islands. Iraq in the past has claimed ownership of these islands. They are not inhabited, but studies show they lie atop oil reserves. Most of Kuwait's other islands are small and uninhabited, although some are used as fishing spots or as popular weekend destinations offering coral reefs and white sands.

The only island with any significant population is Failaka. It is located south of Bubiyan at the mouth of Kuwait Bay, about twelve miles northeast of Kuwait City. Failaka is unique in that it contains ruins dating back to the fourth century B.C., when Alexander the Great founded a Greek colony on the island. In addition, Failaka's soil is fertile and it has fresh underground water, making it a prime site for agriculture. After the discovery of oil in Kuwait, many inhabitants of Failaka maintained their residency but abandoned farming and fishing to work in government jobs, and the island became a prime beach resort. However, when Iraqi forces invaded Kuwait in 1990, they planted mines on much of the island, causing most residents to abandon Failaka; since then, the island has been uninhabited.

SOURCES OF FRESHWATER

Kuwait has no permanent rivers, streams, or lakes and thus has an almost total lack of freshwater. Sudden rainstorms from October to April may fill desert basins with water temporarily, but they quickly go dry again. Kuwait once relied on oases, areas where water from underground springs or artesian wells reaches the surface, but these have largely disappeared; today only one oasis remains, in an area south of Kuwait City.

Since the population began to grow in the 1950s, Kuwait has depended on a few underground water reservoirs and successful desalination programs (converting saltwater to freshwater) to provide drinking water for its people and

A worker at a desalination plant in Doha drinks water from a cooler. Kuwait relies on desalination plants to supply its citizens with drinking water.

freshwater for industry and other uses. Today Kuwait boasts some of the world's most sophisticated desalination plants. Most facilities are in the Doha area; in May 2004 the government approved a contract to build the Middle East's largest desalination plant, in the northern city of Sabiya. Slated for completion in January 2007, the plant will produce 227,000 tons of potable water daily, enough to supply 600,000 people.

CLIMATE

Kuwait's desert climate is hot, dry, and windy. The average daily temperature is about 90 degrees Fahrenheit, but temperatures in the summer can reach 125 degrees Fahrenheit—in the shade. Summers are not only hot but long, lasting from May through October. Also, during June and July, warm and dry northwesterly winds blow, creating numerous and frequent sandstorms. Beginning in August and continuing into September, the heat is accompanied by very high humidity, which makes conditions even more unbearable.

During the relatively short winters, which last from November through February, temperatures drop to an average of about 56 degrees Fahrenheit. At night, temperatures can be even cooler, sometimes (although rarely) even dropping to freezing. Winter and early spring (a short season in March and April) are also the times when it rains in Kuwait, although rainfall averages less than five inches per year. The amount of precipitation, however, varies widely, with some years experiencing very little rain and other years significantly more.

The heat and aridity of the climate has inspired the Kuwaiti government to create a more hospitable environment by developing areas of lush, green landscaping around the country. One such area is a forty-acre artificial island, Green Island, created in 1988 off Kuwait City's waterfront. Connected to land by an 825-foot concrete causeway, Green

 ## KUWAIT'S PEARL BEDS

Although Kuwait has not had a thriving pearl industry since the 1930s, it holds a nine-day festival each August to commemorate its maritime history, including the tradition of pearl diving. During the festival, experienced divers and students go on pearl diving expeditions to reenact the dangerous and difficult occupation. The reenactors give up the luxuries of modern life for a week of living on wooden boats that are replicas of original pearl boats. During the week they dive for pearls in the same way their ancestors did. They wear the same loincloths (which depict their rank), eat the same diet of fish and dates, and make repeated dives to the seabed, where they pluck oysters and put them in wooden boxes, which are hauled to the surface by other crew members. Divers then swim to the surface as quickly as they can, and the oysters are pried open to reveal their pearl gems. The natural pearls are formed from hardened secretions over worms or other foreign material that enters the oyster shells.

Pearl diving can be extremely hazardous. Many early pearl divers died from drowning, shark bites, poisonous fish, and malnutrition during a season that lasted from May until September. Today, safety precautions are taken to ensure that dives are made in safe waters of limited depth. Despite these restrictions, however, in 2003 divers brought back forty-five thousand oysters containing more than forty small pearls and a large one that was worth about $13,200. During an earlier festival in 1993, divers found one oyster containing seventeen pearls, one worth $50,000.

Island features a swimming pool, restaurants, a children's play area, a concert amphitheater, and fifty thousand shrubs and plants that make it appear to be an oasis of green.

PLANTS, ANIMALS, AND THE EFFECTS OF WAR

Kuwait's desert conditions support a limited range of plants and animals. As historian Longva puts it, "With no surface water, almost no rainfall, and extreme climatic conditions, Kuwait's physical environment was scarcely amenable to animal and vegetable life."[3] Kuwait's plants, therefore, are primarily species that are extremely drought tolerant and, in the coastal salt marshes, salt tolerant. In the sand dunes near the coast, for example, low-growing perennial shrubs and annual grasses can be found. Desert vegetation is also mostly clumps of perennial desert grass. However, following the rains in late winter and early spring, the desert sprouts colorful flowers and bright green grass. During this part of the year, herds of sheep, goats, and camels graze in certain parts of the desert where grasses are abundant. The vegetation soon fades in the increasing heat, leaving a very muted color palette.

Kuwait's animal population, likewise, comprises species that can survive extremes of temperature. Thirty-eight types of reptiles have been recorded, mostly lizards and snakes. Smaller mammals can also be found, such as gerbils, rabbits, and foxes. Most abundant, however, are insects—crickets, dragonflies, and cockroaches—as well as scorpions and spiders. The most attractive insects are butterflies; several varieties are native to Kuwait, and the best season in which to observe them is spring.

Perhaps the most abundant animal life in Kuwait is birds. Kuwait has only a few native bird species, but some three hundred species

A cormorant sits covered in oil during the Gulf War. Oil spills during the war killed thousands of birds and other animals.

have been identified in the country because many flocks of nonnative birds migrate to the area during the wetter, cooler months, landing and nesting on Kuwait's islands and shores and feeding in its shallow waters, which are rich in marine life. Eagles, cormorants, terns, and wading birds such as brightly colored flamingos find a haven in Kuwait, and so many seagulls roost on one of the smaller islands, Kubbar Island, that it is considered a seagull sanctuary.

The Gulf War, however, devastated much of Kuwait's natural environment. The treads of tanks and other military vehicles, the encampment of troops, and the carnage of battle destroyed fragile desert plants and disrupted animal habitats. The retreating Iraqis also sabotaged Kuwait's vast oil facilities, spilling oil into the desert and into the Persian Gulf; as much as thirty thousand barrels of oil spouted daily from some damaged wells. The oil formed lakes in the deserts, attracting birds that landed on the sticky surface and were coated with lethal crude oil. The oil spills killed birds, fish, and other wildlife, polluted the soil, and led many to worry about contamination of some of the country's scarce underground water supplies. Iraqi forces also set many oil wells on fire, creating clouds of noxious soot that blanketed the country and had long-lasting adverse effects on wildlife, plants, and marine habitats.

POPULATION AND CITIES

Because of the extreme heat, most of Kuwait's population lives along the coast, where it is cooler than it is inland. Kuwait's cities are all grouped in the coastal belt, and most people are urban dwellers. Indeed, even Kuwait's Bedouin nomad population has largely settled into permanent residences in these urban areas. Kuwaitis themselves distinguish between "inner" Kuwait, referring to coastal urban areas, where political attitudes are more likely to be progressive or liberal, and "outer" Kuwait, referring to areas a bit farther inland, where more conservative Bedouin and tribal influences remain strong.

The country's capital, Kuwait City, is located at the mouth of Kuwait Bay, on the Persian Gulf. It is a small city, with a population of only about 32,600 within the city limits. However, most of Kuwait's people live in the capital's suburbs and a few outlying towns; the population of this broad metropolitan area is about 1,709,800. Two of Kuwait's largest cities are located here: Salmiyah (pop. 152,000), just southeast of Kuwait City and known for its bazaars and shopping malls, and Hawalli (pop. 96,000), also part of the metropolis near the capital.

Kuwait's total population, according to U.S. government estimates in 2004, is about 2.3 million. This figure is rising rapidly, however; Kuwait has a high birth rate, in part due to the high income status of most Kuwaiti citizens and the government's encouragement of large families. As a result of this baby boom, the majority of Kuwait's population today is young, with approximately 65 percent of the population under the age of 25.

Also notable is the fact that almost 1.3 million of Kuwait's residents, or more than half of the country's total population, are noncitizens, mostly foreign workers whose numbers mushroomed after World War II when the oil industry created a demand for skilled and unskilled labor that could not be met by Kuwait's small native population. Over time, educated Kuwaitis replaced foreigners at the highest management levels of business and industry, but factors such as the increased incomes of Kuwaiti families and the nonparticipation of women in the workforce combined to support a

Pictured is an oil refinery outside Kuwait City. Kuwait's oil reserves represent nearly 10 percent of the world's oil deposits.

continuing need for lower-paid outside labor, even up to the present day.

This foreign workforce was at first primarily Arab, including many Palestinians, Jordanians, and Egyptians. Many of these Arab workers, however, were expelled after the Persian Gulf War because their leaders (and some workers themselves) had sided with Iraq. Today many of Kuwait's foreign laborers come from Asian countries such as India, Pakistan, Bangladesh, Sri Lanka, and the Philippines. This foreign population enjoys no political or social rights. They have little chance of becoming citizens, even though many spend their entire lives in Kuwait, because Kuwait reserves citizenship for those who can establish proof of their family's residency prior to 1920.

Kuwait's population also includes about 120,000 stateless Arabs known as the Bidoon (literally, "without"). The Bidoon, mostly Bedouins, claim they have lived in Kuwait for generations, but the government maintains they are recent immigrants who should not be granted full citizenship.

NATURAL RESOURCES: OIL

Kuwait's only significant natural resource today is oil; as writer Frank A. Clements puts it, "The name Kuwait is now synonymous with oil."[4] This oil and its by-product, natural gas, are the country's main economic products. In fact, although it is small in size, Kuwait ranks third in the Middle East in known oil reserves; only its much larger neighbors, Saudi Arabia and Iraq, have more oil than Kuwait. Kuwait sits above an estimated 96.5 billion barrels of oil reserves, more than 9 percent of the world's total oil deposits. Without the economic profits available from oil, the Kuwaiti government would have a difficult time supporting a substantial population in the otherwise arid and barren country.

Most of Kuwait's oil production is located in the south at Burgan and surrounding fields. Other producing areas include two northern fields (Rawdhatain and Sabiryah) and two fields south of Burgan (Minagish and Umm Qudayr). In addition, by agreement, Kuwait and its southern neighbor, Saudi Arabia, share oil from an area on the border of the two countries called the Saudi-Kuwaiti Neutral Zone. Kuwait's net oil export revenues in 2004 were projected to be approximately $17 billion.

OTHER INDUSTRY

Before oil became the country's chief export, Kuwait's economy relied largely on sea trade, boatbuilding, pearl diving, and fishing. At one time, in fact, Kuwait was known throughout the world for its pearls, valuable gems that form in oyster shells on the sea floor. The Persian Gulf once had vast oyster beds; Kuwaiti pearl divers collected the oysters and brought them to the surface, where they were opened to expose the pearls. The pearl industry, however, disappeared in the 1930s. A worldwide depression lowered the demand for the gems; at about the same time, Japan developed a process for cultivating pearls under artificial conditions, allowing them to be manufactured and sold much more cheaply. Other industries, such as sea trading and fishing, never produced substantial earnings; however, they continue to play a minor role in Kuwait's economy.

Kuwait has made efforts, somewhat unsuccessfully, to diversify its economy to include products other than oil. Banking

KUWAIT'S OIL DEPOSITS

Kuwait's enormous oil reserves are spread across the country. Most of Kuwait's oil is located in southern Kuwait in the Greater Burgan area; this area includes the Burgan, Magwa, and Ahmadi fields and holds 70 billion barrels of reserves. Indeed, Burgan is considered the world's second largest oil field; only Saudi Arabia's Ghawar field has produced more oil since 1938. Kuwait's Rawdhatain, Sabiryah, and Minagish fields, all of which have been producing since the 1950s, also have large known reserves (respectively, 6 billion, 3.8 billion, and 2 billion barrels). Another oil field, discovered in 1984, the South Magwa field, is estimated to hold at least 25 billion barrels of oil, and as recently as November 2000, Kuwait announced the discovery of significant additional amounts at the Sabiryah field. Moreover, the Neutral Zone area, which Kuwait shares with Saudi Arabia, is estimated to contain 5 billion barrels of reserves, half of which belong to Kuwait.

One of Kuwait's oil fields, the Ratqa field, is somewhat controversial. It was once believed to be an independent reservoir but later was found to be a southern extension of Iraq's great Rumalia oil reserves. Before its 1990 invasion of Kuwait, Iraq accused Kuwait of stealing billions of dollars of Rumaha oil and refused to share it. After the Gulf War, the United Nations established a legal border in this area, giving Kuwait all eleven oil wells that it had developed at Ratqa. These wells produce about forty thousand barrels of oil per day.

and finance were two areas the government hoped to develop. Kuwait's first bank was established in 1941, followed by several other banks and financial companies, all government-owned. These institutions thrived initially, particularly during the 1970s when large oil revenues provided funds to many private individuals and businesses, creating a need for financial services. However, a huge crash of Kuwait's stock market in 1982 shook the nation's economy and put most of Kuwait's banks and financial institutions out of business. The industry still has not recovered.

Some efforts were also made to promote non-oil manufacturing, in areas such as electrical and water distillation plants, small manufacturing companies, and communications industries. So far the government has provided only minimal support to these industries, and they have yet to form a large part of Kuwait's economy. Efforts also have been made to encourage local agriculture, using desalinated water from huge state-run waterworks. Like other non-oil industries, however, farming is limited. It is also unlikely to grow substantially given Kuwait's climate and lack of abundant fresh water. In the absence of local industry, Kuwait imports many products, including food and consumer goods, and continues to depend almost exclusively on oil sales and investment income. For now and the foreseeable future, Kuwait's economy is expected to remain oil-based.

An oil pump draws oil from a deposit in northern Kuwait. Although efforts have been made to diversify the economy, Kuwait remains dependent on revenue from oil sales.

History of a "Little Fort"

Kuwait's history stretches back eight thousand years to the Middle Stone Age. In ancient times, Kuwait was populated by Bedouin nomads, herders and traders who roamed the deserts. Modern Kuwait, however, evolved only after nomadic people began settling along the Gulf coast, where one family—the al-Sabah—emerged as the area's leaders. Indeed, the name Kuwait, simply translated, means "little fort" and probably refers to this first coastal settlement. Kuwait's history from that point on is the story of how a tiny sheikdom evaded conquest by larger powers and established itself, largely because of its oil resources, as an independent Middle East nation.

Ancient Kuwait

Little is known of the earliest inhabitants of the area now called Kuwait. Geologists believe that millions of years ago the land in Arabia (the ancient term for the broad peninsula of which Kuwait is a part) was covered by a vast blanket of ice that had advanced from Europe. Beginning about ten thousand years ago, the sheet of ice gradually retreated, leaving behind green and well-watered marshes and grasslands. With climatic change, the grasslands slowly dried and evolved into deserts. Lacking fossils or other evidence, scientists speculate that the ancient peoples who inhabited these pre-desert areas probably adapted to the drying conditions by seeking out lands that would support crops and by learning to domesticate, breed, and shepherd animals.

Some primitive people congregated near large rivers in Mesopotamia, a fertile area northwest of Kuwait, now Iraq, that is considered the cradle of the world's civilization. This group gradually developed agriculture and permanent settlements. Archaeological evidence also suggests that an ancient civilization lived on the coast of Kuwait and on the island of Failaka at the entrance to Kuwait Bay. Many other primitive people, however, remained nomads who lived in the deserts Arabia (including Kuwait and Saudi Arabia), wandering with their herds of camels, sheep, and goats from one oasis to the next.

These desert nomads were called the Bedouin. As writers H.V.F. Winstone and Zahra Freeth explain, the Bedouin "were uncompromisingly [nomadic], untouched by foreign ideas, unfamiliar with any world except their own."[5] They stayed within their broad home territories and were loyal strictly to their family and tribe. Winstone and Freeth describe the appearance of the Bedouin tribal people: "The men were spare and wiry in physique, with strong aquiline noses set in brown faces. . . . The womenfolk . . . were clothed in long coloured gowns, their heads draped in black, and their faces covered with the burga or mask with two eyeholes. They remained veiled even when attending to the cooking or household tasks."[6] The Bedouin were known for their hospitality, pride, honor, courage, and endurance.

The desert Bedouin had few possessions other than their animals; they carried only a few necessities such as tents,

A Kuwaiti Bedouin tends to his herd of sheep at sunset. The Bedouin keep sheep as a secondary food supply and as a source of wool.

rugs, quilts, cooking utensils, camel saddles, and at least one rifle for defense. Typically, the tribes of Arabia invested almost exclusively in camels, which were considered indispensable for life in the desert. Camels carried heavy loads and were the primary source of milk for food and dung for fuel; they also took the nomad warrior into battle and enabled him to travel long distances on the desert sands. Among the Bedouin, therefore, the camel became a symbol of status and security. Tribes of the desert sometimes went to war with each other to acquire the other side's camels. The Bedouin owned sheep and goats as a secondary food supply. Bedouin women also wove goat's hair and sheep's wool into traditional long, low black tents and other items.

The culture of the Bedouin and other peoples of Arabia was greatly affected when the prophet Muhammad, who lived from A.D. 571 to 632, founded the religion of Islam, the

A Bedouin mother poses with her two children. The traditional way of life of the Bedouin has changed little over thousands of years.

basis for all Arab culture in the Middle East. Bedouin tribes and armies of Muslims—followers of Islam—spread the religion throughout Arabia, including Kuwait, where traditional patterns of life changed little over the next thousand years.

EARLY SETTLEMENTS

Kuwait's modern history began in the early 1700s when a small fishing settlement was founded by a group of Bedouin people known as the Bani Utub (in Arabic, "people who wander"). The Bani Utub were members of the Anaiza tribe, a nomadic people from central Arabia, what is today Saudi Arabia. The Utub were forced from their homeland by a severe drought and, after much traveling, reached the protected harbor today known as Kuwait Bay. Because this area also had a good supply of freshwater, the Bani Utub stayed. The name of the settlement, Kuwait, means "little fort" in Arabic and is believed to refer to a small fort built to guard the early settlers.

The Utub gave up their nomadic life to become fishermen, shipbuilders, and sailors. The small community also quickly became a center for commerce, allowing many early inhabitants to become traders and merchants. The coastal area and its fine harbor provided a stable and strategic trading hub for goods being sent to and from Arabia; it was both a depot for camel caravans transporting goods to inland desert areas and a seaport for longer-range trade to other regions and countries, particularly India. As Longva explains,

> In 1758 large caravans of five thousand camels and a thousand men passed through Kuwait. . . . The pride of Kuwait, meanwhile, rested in its *booms,* the larger deep-sea vessels that [sailed] between Kuwait in the north and Oman, India, and East Africa in the south. The cargo of the *booms* that set sail for the south in November each year was mainly Iraqi dates, ghee [clarified butter] and Arabian horses; they returned in the spring, loaded with spices, rice, sugar, manufactured goods, and wood for boat-building from India, coffee from Yemen, tobacco and dried fruits from Persia, and mangrove poles for house-building from East Africa.[7]

The early inhabitants of Kuwait also worked in pearl diving, a seasonal industry that flourished from May until September

Fishing boats lie anchored along the shore in Kuwait Bay. Kuwait's modern history began in the early 1700s when Bedouin fishermen established a settlement in the bay.

and yielded beautiful gems that were in high demand in Iraq, India, and Europe. As described by an observer:

> Each man works naked except for a loin-cloth and leather protection over his fingers; the diver descends rapidly to the bottom on a heavy stone which is attached by rope to the boat. His nostrils are stopped by a wooden clip on his nose; he carries a knife to cut the oysters from the bottom, working as fast as he can while his breath lasts; tied round his neck is a small basket to carry his catch. The haulers in the boat above pull up the stone after each dive, and the diver surfaces unaided when he can stay down no longer.[8]

This was a dangerous profession; many divers drowned or were killed by sharks. It also paid very little, barely enough for a diver's family to survive. Nevertheless, it became one of Kuwait's most successful industries; by the beginning of World War I, between ten thousand and fifteen thousand Kuwaitis worked either as divers or as crew members in the industry.

By 1904 the town of Kuwait had about thirty-five thousand residents. Its population included not only original settlers—descendants of the Bani Utub and Kuwaiti nomads—but also Arabs from Iraq and the southern Gulf area, slaves and ex-slaves from Africa, and non-Arab Persians from Iran. Regardless of ethnicity, almost all Kuwaitis were Muslims, followers of Islam.

THE SABAH SHEIKDOM

By the middle of the eighteenth century, one family emerged as the leading political force in Kuwait—the al-Sabah. Because they were good at managing the town's affairs, members of this family were selected by prominent merchants to be Kuwait's early leaders. Their political responsibilities included maintaining the town's security and handling diplomatic relations between the various tribes that traded in Kuwait.

During the rule of the first al-Sabah leader (Sabah I), Kuwait became a province of the powerful Ottoman (Turkish) Empire, which controlled much of the Middle East at that time. In practice, however, the authority of the Ottomans in this part of the world was very weak, and a powerful tribe known as the Bani Khaled was the real ruling force over much of Arabia. The al-Sabah family maintained friendly relations with the tribe and in this way continued to govern Kuwait while gaining protection and security from the Bani Khaled.

Under the long rule of Sabah I's son (Abdallah I), the al-Sabah became the uncontested ruling family of Kuwait. During this period, the al-Sabah survived a challenge from another family, the al-Khalifa, which was resolved when the

 ## THE AL-SABAH RULERS

Kuwait has had a total of thirteen al-Sabah family members as its leaders since its founding as a small settlement in the 1700s. Eleven al-Sabah sheiks ruled Kuwait from 1752 until its national independence in 1961; since then Kuwaiti rulers have been known as emirs.

The current emir, Jabir al-Ahmad al-Jabir al-Sabah, in power since 1977, is now in his seventies. His designated successor is Crown Prince Sheik Saad al-Abdullah al-Sabah. However, the crown prince is in poor health, raising questions and a certain level of tension among Kuwaitis about whether there will be a smooth succession and whether the new emir will provide active leadership in coming years.

al-Khalifa family left Kuwait, eventually settling and becoming the ruling family in a nearby Gulf state, Bahrain. From this point onward, Kuwaitis were led by a ruler, or sheik, from the al-Sabah family. This family became a dynasty; indeed, all of Kuwait's rulers, even into present times, have been members of this family.

OTTOMAN ALLIANCES

In addition to the one-time internal challenge, early al-Sabah rulers were threatened by outside forces—threats that eventually led Kuwait to form closer relations with the Ottoman Empire. During the rule of Abdallah I, for example, the powerful Bani Khalid tribe, which had historically provided protection to Kuwait, faced attacks from followers of religious leader Muhammad Abd al-Wahhab (called the Wahhabis). The Wahhabis advocated a fundamentalist approach to Islam, which condemned all types of luxury or self-indulgence including tobacco, alcohol, prostitution, superstition, music, and dancing. They sought to spread these religious and political reforms throughout Arabia by force. As

Sheik Jabir al-Ahmad al-Sabah speaks to reporters in 2003. The al-Sabah family has ruled Kuwait since the 1700s.

Winstone and Freeth explain, "Men seen smoking in the streets were sometimes shot, women out after dark and suspected of immorality were seized and beaten."[9] The Wahhabis eventually established the modern state of Saudi Arabia. The Bani Khalid repeatedly fought the Wahhabi advance, but during the late 1700s they were defeated. Without the Bani Khalid, Kuwaitis feared they too would soon be conquered by the Wahhabi.

To protect Kuwait from Wahhabi attacks, Abdallah I forged alliances with larger outside powers. In 1775, for example, Abdallah I began a relationship with Britain by helping it with some trading difficulties; in return, Britain helped Kuwait to fight the Wahhabis by supplying cannons and troops. In addition, the next al-Sabah ruler, Abdallah II, formed closer ties with the Ottomans, prompting the Turks to send military forces to Arabia, where they defeated the Wahhabis in 1818. However, Abdallah II soon worried that the Ottomans might gain too much power over Kuwait. To prevent this, he negotiated an arrangement with the Ottoman Empire that established a close friendship while at the same time giving the al-Sabah family complete autonomy in the governing of Kuwait. The next ruler, Abdallah's brother Muhammad, strengthened this Ottoman alliance.

THE BRITISH ERA

Kuwait's alliance with the Ottomans was broken at the end of the nineteenth century during the rule of Sheik Mubarak I (called Mubarak the Great). In the only violent coup in Kuwait's history, Mubarak came to power in 1896 by killing his brothers, Muhammad and Jarrah, whom he believed were too closely aligned with the Ottomans. Mubarak feared, along with many merchants and others in Kuwait, that Muhammad's pro-Ottoman policies might result in a loss of independence for Kuwait. Mubarak believed that only by associating with a Western world power could Kuwait escape Ottoman conquest.

Accordingly, Mubarak quickly made diplomatic contacts with Britain. Britain, which was interested in protecting its trade routes to India from the Ottomans, agreed to provide gunboats to Mubarak as protection against Ottoman rule. Three years later, Britain and Kuwait negotiated a more formal alliance. Under the terms of an 1899 treaty, Britain promised to protect Kuwait from foreign attackers. In exchange, Kuwait agreed to be loyal to Britain and not make agreements with other countries without Britain's consent.

The treaty with Britain placed Kuwait firmly within the British sphere of influence in the Middle East. As Crystal explains, "Kuwait purchased its independence from regional powers [the Ottomans] but only at the price of an ultimately deeper dependence on Britain."[10] After the treaty was signed, for example, Britain sent a political agent to Kuwait to advise the al-Sabah family, sometimes on domestic policy but more often on Kuwait's foreign policy. In most cases Kuwait was obliged to follow this advice or risk destroying relations with Britain.

However, the alliance with Britain also provided valuable benefits to Kuwait. The British sent military aid to Kuwait, protecting it against attacks from neighboring powers in Arabia. When Wahhabi forces, by then under the control of Saudi Arabian leader Ibn Saud, attacked Kuwaiti troops in 1920, for ex-

MUBARAK THE GREAT

Mubarak the Great, who ruled Kuwait from 1896 to 1915, is known as the founder of modern Kuwait. He was raised in the desert and was a tough, proud, and independent man capable of decisive action. He began his career when his brother, Sheik Muhummad, brought him into the government to be in charge of desert security and tribal relations. In May 1896, Mubarak, with his sons Jabir and Salim (both of whom would later become rulers in Kuwait) and his supporters, launched a secret coup that killed Muhammad and Mubarak's other brother, Jarrah. Afterward, Mubarak declared himself Kuwait's new ruler. This violent transfer of power was accepted within Kuwait because many Kuwaitis were dissatisfied with Muhammad, who was viewed as a weak ruler who supported a close relationship with the Ottoman Empire. Under Muhammad's rule, the deserts of Kuwait became lawless, with certain desert tribes raiding and plundering peaceful settlements, and forces cooperating with the Ottomans began plotting an ouster of the al-Sabah ruling family from Kuwait.

Once in power, Mubarak wasted no time in declaring that Kuwait would never submit to Ottoman rule. When the Ottomans sent officials to take control of the port of Kuwait, Mubarak asked Britain for protection. Eventually, after Germany and Russia took an interest in the area, Britain agreed to enter into a formal treaty with Kuwait. This relationship with Britain ensured Kuwait's security in the region, paving the way for its later emergence as an independent nation.

Kuwaiti leaders discuss the location of oil deposits with British officials. Kuwait's relationship with Britain began in 1899, when a treaty between the two nations was ratified.

ample, Britain sent air and sea support that helped Kuwait win an important victory. According to Crystal, this famous battle, the Battle of Jahrah, "established Kuwait's independence from Saudi Arabia and reinforced the city-state's growing national identity."[11] British protection thus provided Kuwait with security and peace, allowing it to grow. These peaceful conditions also helped Mubarak and his successors to stay in power and to increase the power of the ruling sheik. In these ways, the friendship with Britain helped strengthen Kuwait and position it later to become an independent nation.

OIL DISCOVERIES

The discovery and later development of massive crude oil reserves enabled Kuwait to emerge as an economic power and eventually to cut its ties with Britain. Although oil had been seeping from the desert sands for many centuries, the extent of oil reserves in Kuwait was not confirmed until 1938, two years after drilling began. The oil exploration was made possible when Kuwait's ruler at the time, Sheik Ahmad al Jabir al-Sabah, signed an agreement in 1934 giving drilling rights to the Kuwait Oil Company (KOC), a jointly owned British-American enterprise. KOC began drilling operations in 1936 but did not strike oil until it moved its activities to an area south of Kuwait Bay. KOC's second drilling attempt, in 1938, struck a gusher in an area that came to be known as the Burgan oil field, the second-largest oil field ever discovered. A bottle of oil from this well was presented to an overjoyed Sheik Ahmad, who soon began receiving a small but regular income from oil production.

Oil rescued Kuwait from an economic crisis that had been caused by two earlier economic blows. The first was an embargo imposed by Saudi Arabia in 1923 after the Battle of Jahrah that prohibited Saudis from buying Kuwaiti goods, a policy that disrupted Kuwait's trading for more than a decade. The second economic blow was even more severe—Japan's development of cultured pearls, which significantly lowered the price of Kuwait's pearls, one of its main exports. By 1930, these two developments had thrown Kuwait's economy into a bad recession. The oil discoveries provided great hope that Kuwait could soon stabilize its economy and regain a measure of prosperity.

Oil prosperity for Kuwait, however, was delayed by the start of World War II. Britain, on whom Kuwait depended for development of its oil, suspended oil production in the country for the duration of the war. In 1946, after the war ended, Kuwait finally began to develop its oil industry, export its oil, and reap the rewards of its oil bounty. By 1947, KOC was producing an astonishing 16.2 million barrels of oil per year.

THE MAJLIS MOVEMENT

Although the new oil revenue eventually solved Kuwait's economic crisis, it also created a new political crisis for the country. In the past, the power of the al-Sabah rulers had been limited because it was dependent on tax revenues from the merchant class. The merchants could withhold taxes as leverage to pressure ruling sheiks on political issues. Unlike taxes, however, oil revenues came directly from the oil companies, cutting the merchants out of the loop and giving the ruling family much greater power. Concerned about Kuwait's rulers gaining absolute power, merchants organized in 1938 to demand reforms in the way Kuwait was governed, a struggle later called the Majlis Movement. They asked, for example, to be involved in deciding which member of the al-Sabah family would become the next ruler, for greater input into policy matters, and for an expansion of health and education programs for Kuwaiti citizens.

Kuwait's ruler rejected their demands, but the merchants did not back down. With the support of Sheik Ahmad's cousin Abdallah Salim, they formed the first Kuwaiti legislative body, called the Council (or *Majlis*), and pressured Sheik Ahmad to abide by its laws. When the Council demanded that its members, not the ruling sheik, receive oil revenues, Sheik Ahmad shut down the legislative body by military force. In its place, he established a purely advisory council.

The A1-Sabah rulers thus remained the sole recipients of Kuwait's oil profits. Even though it failed, the Majlis Movement provided Kuwait with its first taste of democracy.

OIL PROSPERITY

The leader who presided over Kuwait's postwar rise to wealth and prosperity was Sheik Abdallah Salim. In tribute to his role in developing Kuwait into a modern, wealthy state, the anniversary of the date he took the throne, February 25, 1950, is celebrated as a national holiday.

Sheik Abdallah used the flood of new oil revenues to implement an ambitious development plan to turn Kuwait into a modern power. He approved major construction contracts to build roads, schools, and hospitals; developed large areas of previously worthless desert lands; and created generous health, education, and welfare programs for Kuwaiti citizens. Abdallah also provided Kuwaitis with jobs, creating a large government bureaucracy. As scholar Simon C. Smith notes, "Attractive and abundant employment opportunities were . . . provided, so

A Kuwaiti villager leads his fully laden camel along a paved road in 1945.

much so that by 1955 55.6 per cent of the labour force was employed by the government."[12] These programs spread Kuwait's oil wealth throughout its citizenry, and their popularity helped ensure support for continued al-Sabah rule.

Sheik Abdallah's spending programs, however, had unforeseen consequences. First, because Kuwait's population was limited in size and lacked many necessary skills, the ambitious projects required hiring hundreds of thousands of foreign workers, both skilled and unskilled. These workers eventually outnumbered Kuwaiti citizens and caused numerous housing and social problems. As professor Miriam Joyce describes it, "Foreign workers who could not find lodging with Kuwaiti families lived in shanty towns, built lean-tos against walls and even slept on the streets."[13] Second, the spending programs were sometimes inefficiently designed or managed, wasting large sums of Kuwait's money and bringing the country close to bankruptcy by the early 1950s. Since British firms contracted for and supervised many of the initial Kuwaiti construction projects, this situation eventually led Kuwait to reevaluate its relationship with Britain.

INDEPENDENCE FOR KUWAIT

Although the discovery of oil in Kuwait increased its value to Britain, Kuwait increasingly saw Britain as an unnecessary drain on its resources. Sheik Abdallah came to believe that British firms were fleecing Kuwait for its oil wealth, leading him to halt spending and expel British companies from the country. Abdallah also began to resent British political and economic advisors, who he felt were motivated by self-interest in directing Kuwaiti contracts to large British firms. By the mid-1950s, tensions had increased to the point where Britain realized it could no longer control Kuwait.

Finally, on June 19, 1961, Britain granted Kuwait its independence and negotiated a new relationship with the nation's ruler. Negotiations between the two countries ended the treaty of 1899 and replaced it with letters of friendship. Under the new arrangement, Britain gave up all control and influence over Kuwait but continued to maintain friendly relations and even to provide military support to the small country, in exchange for access to Kuwaiti oil.

As soon as independence was officially declared, Sheik Abdallah, who had supported Kuwait's first experiment with

KUWAIT'S CONSTITUTION

Kuwait's constitution was adopted on November 11, 1962, and came into force on January 29, 1963, when the first National Assembly was convened. It is a mix of Western and Arab ideas, combining principles of democracy—such as equality of citizens before the law and freedom of press and assembly—with Islamic law. A few of Kuwait's constitutional provisions, listed on the Kuwait Information Office in India Web site (www.Kuwait-info.com), follow:

Article 2: The religion of the State is Islam, and the Islamic Sharia shall be a main source of legislation.

Article 4: Kuwait is a hereditary Amirate, the succession to which shall be in the descendants of the late Mubarak al-Subah.

Article 6: The system of Government in Kuwait shall be democratic, under which sovereignty resides in the people, the source of all powers.

Article 29: All people are equal in human dignity, and in public rights and duties before the law, without distinction as to race, origin, language or religion.

Article 34: An accused person is presumed innocent until proved guilty in a legal trial at which the necessary guarantees for the exercise of the right of defense are secured.

Article 35: Freedom of belief is absolute. The State protects the freedom of practicing religion in accordance with established customs, provided that it does not conflict with public policy or morals.

Article 37: Freedom of the press, printing and publishing shall be guaranteed in accordance with the conditions and manner specified by law.

Article 44: Individuals shall have the right of private assembly without permission or prior notification, and the police may not attend such private meetings.

Article 50: The system of Government is based on the principle of separation of powers . . . [with legislative power vested in the emir and the National Assembly, executive power in the emir, the Cabinet and the Ministers, and judicial power in the courts].

A bustling scene in Kuwait City is photographed in late 1961, shortly after Kuwait achieved independence from Britain.

representative government during the Majlis Movement, took bold actions to make the new nation more democratic. He established a provisional government and instructed its members to draft a constitution. The document that emerged was viewed by many as remarkable for its embrace of democratic ideals. Although it established Islam as the official religion, it also granted liberties such as freedom of assembly and of the press; barred discrimination based on race, social origin, language, or religion; and called for a separate legislature and court system and for other restraints on the power of the ruling Sheiks. This degree of political freedom was unprecedented in the Persian Gulf region, where most countries were ruled by dictators. The constitution was approved on November 11, 1962, and the first general elections were held the following year to form a permanent legislature, called the National Assembly. With these developments, Kuwait took a great leap—from hereditary tribal rule to a more progressive, more democratic government.

However, perhaps the most extraordinary aspect of Kuwait's history is the fact that it survived for centuries without ever fully giving up its autonomy, or self-governance. Although it was tiny and lacking in military power, through creative diplomacy it successfully negotiated with greater powers that sought to control it, following this road ultimately to independent nationhood.

INDEPENDENT KUWAIT

After gaining independence, Kuwait faced new challenges. Disputes with the neighboring country of Iraq, internal political challenges, regional wars, and, finally, a military invasion of Kuwait by Iraqi troops tested the resolve and ability of Kuwait's leaders to maintain an independent democracy and a stable economy. As it did throughout its early history, Kuwait survived these tests by aligning itself with another great power, this time the United States. Not surprisingly, Kuwait was able to gain this superpower protection largely because of its valuable oil reserves.

A Constitutional Monarchy

Kuwait's government is a constitutional monarchy, a system that provides both for democratically elected representatives and for continued rule by a monarch, in this case a member of the al-Sabah family. Kuwait's hereditary ruler (or emir) acts as head of state and appoints a prime minister to lead the government. The emir and prime minister issue decisions (or decrees) through a decision-making body called the Council of Ministers. The emir selects his successor, called the crown prince, from the ruling family. Thus, as in the past, only members of the al-Sabah family can become rulers of Kuwait.

Kuwait also has a legislature or parliament, known as the National Assembly, made up of fifty members elected by popular vote to serve four-year terms. The Assembly reviews decisions issued by the emir and has the power to overturn them. However, the Assembly's authority is limited in several ways. First, only Kuwaiti citizens are permitted to vote, and citizenship is limited to a small minority of the population. Citizens are defined as adult males whose ancestors were living in Kuwait in 1920, males who have been naturalized citizens for thirty years or more, and their male descendants at

BEDOUIN TRIBES IN KUWAITI POLITICS

Many of Kuwait's National Assembly members are tribal candidates who represent various Bedouin tribes. In 1961, Kuwait granted a large number of Bedouin citizenship, offering them social benefits and housing if they would join the Kuwaiti army. The response from the Bedouin was overwhelming, creating a housing crisis as many desert nomads resettled in Kuwait's cities. The government provided additional housing and loans, allowing many Bedouin to become integrated into Kuwaiti society.

In exchange for this aid, the ruling family sought political loyalty. With government encouragement, many Bedouin tribes ran candidates for the National Assembly. In 1967 the government again allowed tens of thousands of Bedouin to become citizens, again providing jobs, housing, and benefits. As a result, the percentage of Bedouin voters grew from 21 percent in 1963 to 45 percent in 1975. Typically, Bedouin Assembly members have voted conservatively and supported the government, although in recent years many tribalists have joined forces with a group known as the Islamists to uphold traditional and religious values and prevent the further Westernization of Kuwait. Today there are still Bedouin members in Kuwait's National Assembly. Indeed, in the 2003 elections, candidates run by Bedouin tribes won 26 of the 50 seats in the Assembly.

age twenty-one. Second, although various political groups exist, formal political parties are not permitted in Kuwait, hampering organized political activity. Finally, the emir retains important powers—the power to reject laws passed by the Assembly and to dissolve the parliament. The emir has taken the latter action three times in Kuwait's modern history when the National Assembly became critical of government policies.

In contemporary Kuwait, therefore, the ruling emir retains considerable power. Kuwait's constitutional monarchy is thus unlike Great Britain's, whose royal ruler's role is primarily that of a figurehead. Nevertheless, as Crystal explains, "The assembly plays a prominent role in raising issues of public importance, reviewing and challenging government policies and programs, and responding to constituent concerns. It helps give Kuwait a much more open and public political life than that in other gulf states."[14]

In addition to the official government, Kuwait continues to exercise an informal, traditional process of political debate called the *diwaniya*—weekly meetings at the homes of prominent men where government issues are discussed. Decisions reached by consensus in these groups are passed along to other meetings and eventually to ruling authorities. This system provides another way for male Kuwaitis to provide input into the political process, especially during periods when the national legislature has been suspended by the emir.

THE PRODEMOCRACY MOVEMENT

Soon after its election in 1963, Kuwait's new National Assembly asserted its right to challenge the emir's policies. Some Assembly members immediately (but unsuccessfully) urged the emir to abandon Kuwait's reliance on Britain for defense and instead join a new, controversial Arab coalition formed by Egypt and Syria called the United Arab Republic. The following year, Assembly members opposed the emir's Council of Ministers, alleging that some of its members were involved in business activities in violation of the constitution. In response, the emir formed a new Council, showing great deference to the legislative body.

Again in 1971 and 1975, elections produced a confrontational National Assembly. Indeed, in 1976, criticism of the ruling emir, Sabah Salim, prompted him to dissolve the Assembly and suspend parts of Kuwait's constitution that guaranteed public assembly and free speech. Elections for a

U.S. president John F. Kennedy (right) meets with a Kuwaiti ambassador in 1962.

new assembly were not held until 1980, after a new emir (Jabir Ahmad) had come to power. After members of the National Assembly began attacking members of the ruling family in 1986 for their handling of a 1982 Kuwaiti stock market crash, Sheik Jabir also suspended the legislative body.

The emir's 1986 suspension of the Assembly led to protests, continuing demands for greater democracy, and a lengthy period of political turmoil. Members of the disbanded Assembly, joined by merchants and other Kuwaitis, organized to call for the legislature and constitution to be reinstated. This effort, called the Prodemocracy or Constitutional Movement, spread throughout Kuwait, largely through the traditional *diwaniya* meetings. When the emir tried to break up the meetings using tear gas and police dogs, the movement widened into large antigovernment demonstrations, resulting in violent confrontations with police. Finally, to defuse the situation, the emir changed tactics and announced he would create a new legislative body. However, the new National Council, with fifty elected members and twenty-five appointed members, was less representative than the old legislature and was given only advisory, rather than legislative, powers. In protest, the opposition boycotted the 1990 elections for the new National Council.

THREATS FROM IRAQ

Despite its new independent government, Kuwait remained dependent on Britain for military support and protection. Indeed, just days after Kuwait's June 19, 1961, declaration of independence, Kuwait's autonomy had been directly challenged by one of its neighbors, Iraq. Iraqi premier Abdul Karim Qassem announced that all of Kuwait was part of Iraq. Qassem's announcement renewed Iraq's historical claim to Kuwait—a claim based on the fact that Kuwait was once a part of the Ottoman province of Basra, which later became the state of Iraq. Kuwait, fearing that Iraq would soon send troops to enforce its claim, asked for military aid from Britain. The British responded by sending close to seven thousand troops to protect the small country.

Kuwait realized, however, that it needed to expand its network of support beyond Britain in order to exist as an independent country and prepare for the day when the British were no longer inclined to defend Kuwait. Kuwait's diplomats therefore established contacts throughout the Arab world, seeking admittance to an alliance of Arab nations called the Arab League and seeking to replace the British troops with an Arab or United Nations force. These efforts succeeded when Kuwait was admitted to the Arab League in July 1961; the League provided a security force that soon replaced British troops. The presence of the security force temporarily suppressed Iraqi claims to Kuwait, although relations with Iraq continued to be threatening until 1963,

when a new Iraqi regime came to power and formally recognized Kuwait's independence.

Kuwait's diplomatic achievement in gaining protection from Arab states was a potent symbol that Kuwait was changing from a small sheikdom and British protectorate to an Arab power that had to be respected as an independent nation. Yet the episode also reminded Kuwait of its continuing vulnerability and its need to rely on other countries for its defense.

AMERICAN PROTECTION FOR KUWAIT

As anticipated, Britain's influence in Kuwait receded during the 1970s and 1980s. Following a period of neutrality, Kuwait began to turn increasingly to the United States for support and protection. At first Kuwait maintained friendly relations with both Cold War superpowers, the Soviet Union and the United States. The United States and Kuwait differed, however, on certain critical issues, especially the issue of Arab/Israeli relations, with the United States supporting Israel and Kuwait supporting Arab Palestinians' campaign for an independent Palestinian state.

The Iran-Iraq War (1980–1988) proved to be the tipping factor, pushing Kuwait toward a closer relationship with the United States. Early in the conflict, attacks from Iran made Kuwait's vulnerability clear. In 1981, for example, Iranian

Armed Kuwaiti soldiers conduct a training exercise in the desert near the Iraqi border in 1961, when Iraq threatened to invade Kuwait.

forces bombed Kuwaiti oil installations in response to Kuwait's support of Iraq. In 1984, after Iraq began attacking commercial vessels in the Gulf to keep them from reaching Iranian ports, Iran retaliated by firing missiles at Kuwaiti and Saudi tankers and threatening to close the Strait of Hormuz. Kuwait depended on these vital shipping lanes for its oil exports. Two years later, Iranian troops occupied Iraq's Faw peninsula, close to Kuwait's borders, adding to Kuwaiti insecurity. In response to these threats, Kuwait's emir sought protection from both the Soviets and the United States. Although the Soviets also came to Kuwait's aid, the United States, concerned about disruption of the world's oil supplies, agreed to place eleven Kuwaiti ships under U.S. naval protection.

This assistance from America allowed Kuwait safely to resume its oil shipments, but the war ended in 1988 with no clear victor. Kuwait continued to refuse to allow the United States to build military bases in the country or to have access to Kuwaiti military facilities.

THE 1990 IRAQI INVASION AND THE PERSIAN GULF WAR

Kuwait's resistance to a U.S. military presence ended suddenly in 1990 with the Iraqi invasion of Kuwait. The crisis

Thick clouds of smoke envelop a Kuwaiti oil tanker hit by an Iranian rocket in 1987 during the Iran-Iraq War.

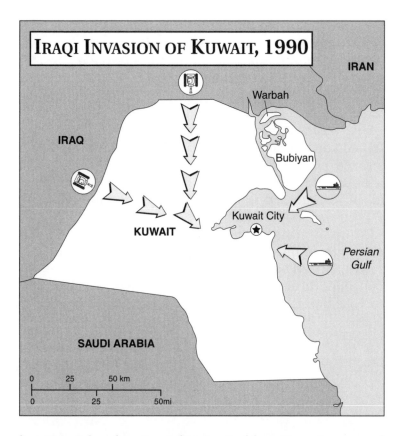

began in July, when Iraqi dictator Saddam Hussein accused Kuwait of driving down the price of Middle East oil by over-producing, in violation of limits set by the Organization of Petroleum Exporting Countries (OPEC). He also claimed that Kuwait was tapping Iraqi oil fields on the Kuwait-Iraq border at Rumalia. Saddam was angered too by Kuwaiti demands that Iraq repay about $13 billion borrowed from Kuwait to finance the Iran-Iraq War.

Iraq demanded that Kuwait cancel Iraq's war debts, give up the Rumalia oil field, lease its offshore islands, and grant Iraq a $10 billion loan. Finally, Saddam disputed the location of the Kuwait-Iraq border and revived Iraq's claim to all of Kuwait. In short, Iraq, which had been crippled economically by its prolonged war with Iran, saw in Kuwait the answers to its problems.

On August 2, after Kuwait refused to meet Iraq's demands, Hussein sent one hundred thousand troops across the border in a largely unopposed invasion. A week later, Iraqi occupiers declared that Kuwait was now a part of Iraq. Iraqi troops began what Joyce has called a "reign of terror" designed to intimidate the population. Joyce relates, "At Kuwait University, in the building that housed the faculties of law and arts, the Iraqis set up a detention and interrogation center. They engaged in murder and in kidnapping."[15] Iraqi forces also demolished Kuwaiti buildings; looted and ransacked industrial and residential areas; destroyed electrical and water desalination plants; stole Kuwaiti cars, cash, and museum treasures; and sabotaged all of Kuwait's oil wells. Within a short time, much of Kuwait was simply ruined.

Kuwait's armed forces, which numbered only about twenty thousand men, were no match for the superior Iraqi forces, though many Kuwaitis bravely resisted the Iraqi occupation. The emir and members of the al-Sabah family fled to neighboring Saudi Arabia, where they formed a govern-

Kuwaiti children celebrate Liberation Day on February 26, 2004. The celebration commemorates the date in 1991 when UN forces liberated Kuwait from Iraq's invading army.

ment in exile. Kuwait had no choice but to turn to the United States and the United Nations (UN) for help.

The UN Security Council condemned the invasion and demanded an immediate Iraqi withdrawal. When Saddam did not pull his forces out of Kuwait, a massive UN military operation began. Dubbed Operation Desert Storm, the effort was led by the United States and Great Britain and supported by a broad coalition of European, Russian, and Arab nations. Indeed, in the Arab world, only Jordan and the Palestinians supported Saddam Hussein.

During the ensuing Persian Gulf War, UN coalition forces liberated Kuwait, pushing the Iraqis back to prewar borders and negotiating a cease-fire on March 3, 1991. Kuwaitis were enormously grateful to the United States. According to Joyce, "joyful crowds kissed arriving soldiers . . . [and] Kuwaitis expressed thanks by offering praise to Allah, and shouting 'USA! USA!'."[16] In September 1991 Kuwait and the United States signed a ten-year defense agreement that provided for a continued and enlarged U.S. military presence in Kuwait. Under this agreement, in exchange for an initial payment of $215 million and pledges of further funds, the United States positioned weapons, aircraft, and other equipment in Kuwait and was permitted to use Kuwaiti ports and airfields in emergencies. In addition, the agreement provided for the two nations to conduct joint military exercises in Kuwait. Kuwait wanted U.S. forces to continue to protect it against future Iraqi threats, and the United States wanted to keep Kuwait secure to maintain world access to the country's vast oil supplies. Kuwait's emir was returned to his embattled country, and his government set out to repair the devastation of the war.

ECONOMIC DEVELOPMENT AND POSTWAR CHALLENGES

Although it was short-lived, the conflict had serious adverse effects on Kuwait's economy, society, politics, and environment. Kuwait's prewar economy was growing: Kuwait had achieved control over its oil in 1976, when the government nationalized, or took over ownership, of KOC, the foreign oil company that had first discovered Kuwait's oil reserves. Later, in 1980, Kuwait formed the Kuwait Petroleum Company (KPC), which soon became one of the largest companies in the world. Through KPC, Kuwait was able to expand

A Kuwaiti couple walks past the rubble of a building in Kuwait City destroyed during the Gulf War. With help from foreign corporations, Kuwaitis rebuilt their country very quickly.

and fully control its oil industry and dramatically increase production and refining capabilities. Despite a stock market crash in 1982, threats during the Iran-Iraq War, and a dramatic drop in oil prices in 1986, by the late 1980s Kuwait was one of the richest economies in the region.

The war abruptly ended Kuwait's economic prosperity. The Iraqis had systematically looted and damaged or destroyed homes, businesses, schools, hospitals, roads, ports, and telephone and electrical systems. Hundreds of thousands of Kuwaiti citizens and foreign workers—more than half of Kuwait's population—had fled the country. Perhaps most important, the Iraqis had severely damaged Kuwait's oil industry. During their retreat, Iraqi forces set fire to some seven hundred Kuwaiti oil wells, blazes that consumed four to six million barrels of oil a day and took nine months to extinguish. Eleven million barrels of oil intentionally released from damaged facilities also flowed across Kuwait and into the Gulf, polluting eight hundred miles of coastline. The attacks eliminated Kuwait's main source of income, wasted its oil resources, and caused major environmental damage.

Nevertheless, with heroic assistance from foreign companies, Kuwaitis rebuilt their shattered country with astonishing speed. As early as August 1991, Kuwait was again exporting oil. The government also managed to restore basic services and rebuild structures that had been damaged in the war. By the end of 1991, most of the physical damage was repaired, allowing exiled Kuwaitis to return. The banking system was rescued with an infusion of government funds, and automobiles and other consumer goods were imported in large quantities to replace those lost to the Iraqis. To help individual Kuwaitis hurt by the war, the government paid all government employees (most of the population) wages for the period of the Iraqi occupation. It also forgave billions of dollars of consumer and housing loans and paid each Kuwaiti family that stayed in Kuwait during the war $1,750.

These programs were necessary to rebuild Kuwait, but they were costly. Altogether, officials estimate that the invasion cost Kuwait $66 billion in lost revenues and damage. Money for the recovery came from Kuwait's international investments and caused hefty budget deficits throughout the 1990s. Reconstruction expenses for 1991 alone exceeded Kuwait's income by $10 billion to $20 billion.

The psychological damage caused by the war was even harder to repair. The war increased Kuwaitis' distrust of foreign workers—especially Palestinians, whose leaders had supported Iraq—making them reluctant to readmit even foreigners who had lived in Kuwait for most or all of their lives. About two-thirds of the foreign workers who left during the occupation were not allowed to return, and many who stayed were asked to leave. Not surprisingly, the upheaval left Kuwait with a significant postwar labor shortage. The war also created divisions between Kuwaiti citizens who stayed in Kuwait and those who fled. Many who remained in Kuwait during the occupation resented those who sat out the war comfortably in exile.

POSTWAR POLITICAL STRUGGLES

Much postwar criticism focused on the ruling family for failing to anticipate and prevent the invasion, for leaving Kuwait so quickly, and for corruption and mismanagement of government while in exile and during reconstruction. Thus the rift between the ruling family and the prodemocracy opposition deepened. The emir's absolute control over Kuwaiti funds while in exile angered the opposition and fueled new calls for democratic reforms. As one Kuwaiti, Ahmad al-Khatib, complained, members of the ruling family were "handling Kuwaiti investments as though they were the private property of the [ruling] family, not the people's money."[17]

The prodemocracy opposition, made up of merchants, former assembly members, conservative Muslims (called Islamists), and others, called for the return of the National Assembly as soon as the war ended.

The opposition was strong enough to negotiate a deal with the exiled Kuwaiti government under which the opposition agreed to support the ruling family in exchange for promises from the emir that he would liberalize the government after the war. The steps the emir agreed to take, at a meeting of more than twelve hundred Kuwaitis in October 1990, included restoring Kuwait's original 1962 constitution and its protection of individual liberties, and reinstating the National Assembly, which had been suspended before the war. Following the meeting, the opposition leaders announced their support for the emir: " 'We emphasize that the Kuwaiti people, one and all . . . stand solidly behind our legitimate leadership whose true embodiment is our emir, Sheikh Jabir al-Ahmad al-Sabah, and his Crown Prince, Sheikh Saad Al-Abdullah Al-Sabah.'"[18]

After liberation, however, the ruling family continued to control government policy. Indeed, within hours of the Iraqi withdrawal, the emir declared martial law, giving the military control over the country and continuing the suspension of press and other freedoms. He also strengthened the government's internal security forces, which were then used to arrest, try, and in some cases torture and impose death sentences on Palestinians who had collaborated with the Iraqis. Meanwhile, the emir delayed responding to opposition demands for a new Assembly and elections.

Finally, in 1992, elections were held for a new National Assembly and constitutional rights were restored. During their campaigns, opposition candidates criticized the emir and the al-Sabah family for their previous treatment of the Assembly and argued for greater democracy, a free press, and a more open political system, in which more people would be permitted to participate. The election resulted in victory for the opposition: A majority of the Assembly seats (35 out of 50) went to members who were critical of the emir and the government. Since 1992, the Assembly has asserted itself by actively investigating government conduct, publicly debating important issues, overruling the emir by simple majority, and reviewing laws issued by the emir when the Assembly was not in session. In particular, the Assembly has focused on the rul-

THE ENVIRONMENTAL DISASTER OF THE GULF WAR

The damage to Kuwait's oil facilities by the Iraqis during the Gulf War was one of the largest environmental catastrophes in history. Although firefighters from all over the world helped to snuff out the fires, which had been set by retreating Iraqi forces, they could not prevent the resulting environmental pollution.

The pollution began with a massive oil spill of as much as 11 million barrels of oil. It transformed the Gulf into a slick of oil, stained the desert sands black, and left a smelly, greasy blanket over rocks and shoreline up to a foot deep. Birds became stuck in the thick oil and died by the thousands despite efforts by volunteers to save them. As Iraqi forces retreated, they set fire to more than seven hundred Kuwaiti oil wells, which burned for many months and sent a half-ton of toxic black smoke and pollution into the atmosphere. The oil and smoke wiped out plants, animals, and fish and made it difficult for people to breathe and to see. Despite cleanup efforts, only about 20 percent of the oil was recovered; most of it continues to pollute habitats and underground water supplies. Winds also distributed the air pollutants across Iran, Pakistan, and India. The lasting health and environmental effects of the disaster are still not fully known, but experts say it will take decades, if not much longer, for the Gulf area to recover fully.

Retreating Iraqi troops set fire to a number of Kuwait's oil wells, sending huge amounts of toxic pollution into the atmosphere.

ing family's handling of Kuwait's finances. As author Anthony H. Cordesman writes,

> The Assembly has begun to participate in major budget and resource decisions, and has actively debated corruption and waste in defense spending, the sharing of the nation's wealth, the royal family's management of the Fund for Future Generations and Kuwait's investments, the repayment of debts owed because of the collapse of Kuwait's stock market, the way in which privatization is conducted, and the amount of money that should be spent on military forces.[19]

In addition to monitoring finances, the Assembly in 1994 succeeded in enacting one expansion of democracy: It increased the citizenship rolls by almost one-third, to include the sons of naturalized citizens.

Kuwait's contemporary politics thus became marked by a struggle between those who seek more liberal, democratic values and those who want to impose a more authoritarian form of government.

THE IRAQI THREAT ENDS

In the spring of 2003, an American-led invasion of Iraq and overthrow of Saddam Hussein had a profound effect on Kuwait. Iraq's threats had for years stunted Kuwait's economic growth and made Kuwaitis fear another military invasion. With Saddam gone, as Kuwaiti Zed al-Refai put it, "the nightmare is over and there is psychological relief. . . . The monster is gone and our [economic] future is now secure."[20]

Kuwaitis' newfound confidence was quickly reflected in an economic boom. Within months of the removal of the Iraqi government, the Kuwaiti stock market surged by 80 percent and real estate prices increased by 40 percent. In addition, oil production increased as fields near Iraq were reopened, raising Kuwait's oil production to approximately a million barrels a day. With increased revenues, the government began to approve new public works and other investments. Kuwait also hoped to reap economic benefits from the major reconstruction projects that were planned for Iraq.

Having overcome many challenges since its inception, Kuwait now seems energized and ready to move ahead toward a more stable future.

Religion, Tradition, and Culture

4

Although oil fueled Kuwait's transformation into a prosperous, modern country, the nation's most important cultural influences remain Islam and the beliefs and customs of its Bedouin past. The country's desert roots can still be seen in a culture that honors traditional values and respects religious law. Indeed, almost all Kuwaitis are Muslims, followers of Islam, and respect for tribal culture and values has increased in recent years. These largely conservative values often clash with recently introduced Western and democratic ideas in Kuwait, creating a country full of contradictions.

TRADITIONAL CULTURE AND CUSTOMS

Kuwait's earliest cultural influence was its environment. The desert life shaped customs and character traits that have become closely identified with Arab culture. Largely because of the need to survive in the harsh desert conditions, one important value that developed among the Bedouin was hospitality—offering rest and shelter to travelers. Other character traits such as honor, loyalty, dependability, and bravery also were recognized as important to life in the desert. At the same time, fighting other tribes and raiding their camels were viewed as ways to test men's courage and strength. The influences of these traditional values can be seen in Kuwaiti social customs, which continue to emphasize hospitality, generosity, loyalty, bravery, personal honor, and reputation.

The desert also produced an essentially tribal culture, in which groups of people were forced to work together to survive. This tribal culture tended to exclude those who were not members of the tribe. As writer William Smyth explains,

"In Arabia it was impossible to survive in the desert alone, and so families banded together to find water and move their flocks to new grazing lands. Once they established the necessary resources through collective effort, they guarded them jealously and refused to share them with outsiders."[21] These traditional tribal influences can be seen in various aspects of contemporary Kuwait. For example, as in tribal society, family remains highly important. Also, similar to the way tribes guarded their resources, the Kuwait government closely restricts citizenship to a small group whose ancestors resided in Kuwait and distributes the social benefits from the country's oil wealth only to those in the select group. Foreigners are treated as outsiders, no matter how long they have lived in Kuwait.

In addition, traditional tribal leadership has become a part of contemporary Kuwait. Desert tribes often made important decisions as a group, with one leader or leading family recognized as the most authoritative voice. The leader

A Bedouin family relaxes in their tent. Bedouin cultural practices have evolved to help these desert dwellers to cope with their harsh environment.

was expected to consult with the tribe, and decisions were made by consensus and agreement rather than by strong individual rule. In this way, the al-Sabah family was selected to rule early in Kuwait's history. This tradition of tribal leadership was passed down through the generations to the present day.

THE IMPORTANCE OF ISLAM IN KUWAIT

Another very important contemporary value with Bedouin roots is obedience to religious laws. Islam remains the guiding force behind both government and culture in Kuwait. Unlike Western nations, Kuwait does not separate religion from its social or political life. Instead, Kuwait has an Islamic government where Islam is designated as the official state religion and civil laws are based on religious laws. Indeed, almost 90 percent of Kuwaitis are Muslims, while only a small minority belong to other faiths such as Christianity and Hinduism.

In Kuwait, as well as throughout the Middle East, the two main Muslim sects or branches, the Sunni and the Shia, co-exist, but most Kuwaiti Muslims are Sunni. The most important religious duties for both sects are contained in Islam's "five pillars": (1) *shahada*, an affirmation of faith that must be recited daily ("There is no god but Allah, and Muhammad is his prophet"); (2) *salat*, prayer performed five times a day—at dawn, midday, mid afternoon, sunset, and nightfall; (3) *zakat*, payment of a religious tax to benefit the poor; (4) *sawm*, daytime fasting (refraining from eating, drinking, smoking, and sexual activity) during one month of the year, usually October, called Ramadan; and (5) *hajj*, a pilgrimage to Mecca, which is considered the birthplace of Islam. Lesser pillars of Islam are *jihad*, the eternal struggle for the triumph of the word of God on Earth, and the requirement to do good deeds and to avoid all evil thoughts, words, and actions.

Devout Muslims take these obligations very seriously. It is common to see Kuwaitis kneeling in prayer throughout the day. At noon on Fridays, men gather at Islamic places of worship, called mosques, to pray as a group and hear a sermon from an Islamic religious leader. They are called to prayer through outdoor loudspeakers with the words *Allah u Akbar* (God is great) and *Laa elaaha ella Allah* (There is no god besides God). Women also may go to the mosques, but many

A Kuwaiti man prays in a mosque in Kuwait City. Islam is Kuwait's official religion, although the constitution guarantees freedom of worship.

pray at home. During Ramadan, many Kuwait businesses close for all or part of the day, and those who can afford it do little or no work.

Other basic Islamic principles important to Muslims in Kuwait include those that forbid stealing, lying, adultery, and murder and others that encourage kindness and honoring one's parents. Islam also supports values such as the pursuit of knowledge, the protection of nature, brotherhood among Muslims, and consideration of the welfare of society and the planet as a whole. A typical greeting between Muslims in Kuwait and elsewhere in the Muslim world is *Assalam alaikum* (Peace be with you). Finally, Islam is generally tolerant of other religions, including Christianity. In Kuwait, Christians and followers of other religions are allowed freedom to worship and practice their religion, as long as they do not try to convert Muslims.

ISLAMIC AND KUWAITI LAW

In Kuwait, Islam is the basis for all the country's laws and judicial rulings. Article 2 of Kuwait's 1962 constitution states that "the religion of the state is Islam" and directs that Islamic law, called *sharia*, be "a main source of legislation."[22] The sharia, in turn, is based on the Quran, which is believed to be the word of Allah given through his prophet Muhammad, and the Sunnah, a collection of actions and sayings of Muhammad that are believed to be examples of the Quran's principles. Islamic law also is derived from two other sources, *qiyas*, which is reasoning by analogy (or similar

 KUWAITI CULTURAL PRACTICES

Kuwaiti social customs stem from deeply held cultural and religious values. Foreigners are expected to respect the following customs:

1. Alcohol, pork products, and goods from Israel are banned, and penalties are severe if these items are found in baggage. Never ask for an alcoholic drink; alcohol is forbidden by Islam.

2. Kuwait is a conservative society. Women dress modestly and men do not wear shorts or go without shirts in public.

3. In Kuwaiti society, reputation and honor are highly valued, and it is disrespectful to show impatience or bad temper, to talk loudly, or to embarrass someone publicly. Also, hospitality is a virtue, so visitors should never decline offers of food or drink.

4. Everything closes on Muslim holidays, which include a month of fasting called Ramadan; Ghadir-é Khom (which commemorates the day that the Prophet Muhammed appointed Emam Ali his successor); and Rabi-ol-Avval (the birthday of Muhammed). In addition, Liberation Day (February 26, when Kuwait was liberated from Iraq), although not an official holiday, is treated like one.

5. Bargaining is not common except in souks (bazaars).

6. Although English is generally widely understood, it is greatly appreciated if visitors learn a few words of Arabic.

7. Kuwait uses the metric system for weights and measures.

example) when no clear Islamic principle applies, and *ijma*, which are judgments reached by a consensus (or agreement) of Islamic religious scholars. These scholars express their opinions by issuing fatwas, or religious rulings.

In the absence of a specific legislative provision, Kuwait's civil code directs judges to decide cases according to custom; in the absence of custom, judges are to rely on principles contained in Islamic religious decisions (called *fiqh*). In Islamic courts, as in the United States, defendants are presumed innocent until proven guilty, and the burden of proof falls on the government or the complaining party. Also as in the West, witnesses must testify under oath. For cases involving family law or personal status, courts are divided into three sections—Sunni, Shia, and non-Muslim—and decisions are based on the particular tenets of the principals' religion.

In general, Islamic law says that everything is permitted (*halal*), except for that which is clearly forbidden (*haram*). However, Islam prohibits a wide variety of conduct and contains a number of strict rules. For example, because the family is considered the basis of social life, Islam encourages marriage and forbids celibacy (refraining from sex). Islam also forbids eating pork or meat from an animal that has not been slaughtered according to religious ritual, by bleeding the animal to death. In addition, Muslims may not drink or handle alcohol or drugs.

The reliance on sharia results in some Kuwaiti laws that are very different from those in the West. For example, Kuwaiti law prohibits and criminalizes not only alcohol but extramarital sex and all forms of pornography.

ISLAM, FAMILY VALUES, AND WOMEN'S RIGHTS

Another area where uniquely Islamic influences can be seen in Kuwait is in its laws on family and women's rights. In some ways, men and women are regarded as equal under Kuwaiti law. Women are permitted to drive, travel alone, work, and go to school, and they have freedom to dress as they please. They also may inherit and hold property, work outside the home, and own their own businesses. Once married, husbands are required to support their wives, and a woman may divorce her husband for lack of support as well as other reasons. Non-Muslim women may practice their religion without restraint and are not subject to Islamic religious requirements in areas such as family and personal rights.

On the other hand, Kuwait's personal status laws, dealing with family issues and applicable to Muslims, are based on Islamic law and openly discriminate against women. In family court, for example, the testimony of a Muslim woman witness is given only half the weight of the testimony of a male witness. Family laws require a father's permission for a Muslim woman to marry, no matter what her age, and Muslim women, unlike Muslim men, may not marry a non-Muslim. In addition, Muslim Kuwaiti women may have only one husband, while men legally may have up to four wives. In areas of divorce and child custody, men's rights are much broader than those of women; men, for example, can divorce for virtually any reason, but women must prove specific grounds (such as nonsupport, impotence, long imprisonment, or serious physical or emotional incapacity) before they can dissolve a marriage. Although women have property rights, according to Islam their inheritance is half that of men.

Islam as practiced in Kuwait restricts women's freedoms in other ways as well. Men are viewed by Islam as the head of household, and Kuwaiti women traditionally have been expected primarily to be wives and mothers; in fact, most

Many of Kuwait's laws are based on Islamic teaching and openly discriminate against women.

Kuwaiti women from traditional families like these women at a soccer match must cover their faces with a veil in public.

Kuwaiti females are married by their early twenties. Indeed, despite the freedoms theoretically offered under Kuwaiti laws, many traditional families continue to seclude women from men by prohibiting female members from leaving the family compound alone and insisting that they wear traditional clothing and cover their faces with a veil when in public. Conservative Islamic groups have fought for even greater restrictions. For example, following protests by Islamic activists, Kuwait University segregated its facilities in the 1980s to separate male students from female students.

ISLAM AND WOMEN'S RIGHT TO VOTE

Perhaps the most controversial issue for women in Kuwait is that they are not allowed to vote or hold political or judicial office. The Kuwaiti constitution does not prohibit the female vote, but election laws do. Advocates of women's rights such as Kuwait's oldest women's organization, the Women's Cultural and Social Society, believe that suffrage for women will bring Kuwait into the twenty-first century and empower Arab women by giving them a voice in government. Exclusion of women from the political arena, they argue, treats them as second-class citizens and is merely a way to reinforce outdated tribal culture, where men handle all political matters while women are secluded from society and in charge of children and domestic chores. True Islam, they say, supports equality for women.

Muslims, however, have differing views about this issue. As professors Helen Rizzo, Katherine Meyer, and Yousef Ali explain,

> Various schools of Islamic thought and interpretation found in different geographic regions hold different attitudes towards women's place in society. Among Sunnis in Kuwait, some follow the Saudi Arabian (Najd) school that believes that women must be separated from public life both socially and politically. Others follow the Egyptian (Alazhar) school . . . which believes that women should be more involved politically. Among Shias in Kuwait, some follow the Iraqi (Najaf) school, which does not support women's political involvement. Other Shias follow the Iranian (Qom) school that endorses the growth of Islamic states such as Iran where the constitution guarantees women's political rights.[23]

Shia political organizations generally tend to support the right of women to vote, while the two largest Sunni groups, the Muslim Brotherhood and the Salafis, oppose it.

Supporters of women's right to vote in Kuwait face the strongest opposition from conservative Kuwaitis who

In 2003 Kuwaiti women vote in a symbolic election to protest their lack of voting rights. Woman suffrage remains one of the most divisive issues in Kuwait.

PROMINENT KUWAITI WOMEN

Although women in Kuwait do not yet have the right to vote, many are highly educated, hold important jobs, and are active politically. Several social and cultural organizations for women exist in Kuwait, including the Women Affairs Committee and Kuwait's Union of Women Societies. These organizations and others have actively fought for women's political rights. Kuwait's most prominent women include:

Dr. Rasha al-Sabah   Undersecretary of Higher Education and one of the emir's most trusted advisors. She was named International Woman of the Year for 1996–1997 by the International Biographical Center in Cambridge, England, and has been involved in education, culture, and women's causes.

Nabila al-Mulla   Kuwait's first female ambassador. She was formerly a deputy permanent representative of Kuwait at the United Nations. She currently serves as Kuwait's ambassador to Austria.

Fayza al-Khorafi   A distinguished scholar, professor, and accomplished scientist. She is the first Arab woman to be appointed to a post at an Arab university.

Sara Akba   A petroleum engineer and member of the Kuwait Oil Company since 1981, she helped to extinguish the oil fires following the Gulf War and to clean up one of the worst environmental disasters in history. She received the Global 500 award from the United Nations Environmental Program in recognition of her work.

Badriya al-Awadi   The top legal expert on human rights and women's rights in Kuwait. She holds a PhD in international law, has published more than ten books, and has taught law at Kuwait University for the past seven years. She focuses on literacy and women's legal and political rights.

support traditional women's roles. As Rizzo, Meyer, and Ali concluded from their research, those opposing suffrage tend to be "Sunnis [who] are older, more educated, religiously traditional people."[24] This group has pushed for resumption of Islamic customs such as the wearing of veils by women and closer observance of religious rites and rituals. Departures from Islam, they say, have caused a deterioration of the family and moral crimes such as drug addiction and juvenile delinquency in Kuwait. They also argue that allowing political rights for women would distract them from what the conservatives consider to be women's natural roles under Islam—as wives, mothers, and managers of households. Given the strong Islamic and tribal opposition, the issue of female suffrage is likely to remain controversial in Kuwait.

ISLAM, TERRORISM, AND KUWAITI POLITICS

Like many countries in the Middle East, in recent years Kuwait has experienced an increase in Islamic fundamentalism, a radical form of Islam whose adherents hold extreme religious views. Islamic fundamentalism most often takes the form of opposition to Western culture and Western involvement in the Middle East and calls for a return to more traditional, conservative Islamic values. Militant Islamic extremists endorse violence and terrorism to achieve their goals. Terrorist groups such as al Qaeda have carried out dramatic bomb attacks not only against American and other Western targets but also against Muslim citizens who are working with or viewed to be sympathetic to the United States or other Western countries.

Kuwait has experienced some Islamic terrorist violence, mostly in the 1980s, following the Islamic revolution in neighboring Iran in 1979. Many Shia in Kuwait supported the Iranian revolution and the anti-American sentiment that was its hallmark. The first terrorist attack in Kuwait came on December 12, 1983, when fundamentalist Muslims backed by Iran drove trucks carrying bombs into the U.S. embassy, the French embassy, and a Kuwaiti oil facility, airline terminal, and government office. The attacks killed five people and wounded eighty-six others. In response, the Kuwaiti government made arrests, sentenced six people to death, and imposed prison terms ranging from five years to life. However, this firm government response provoked additional violence, as Iranian-backed radicals launched a series of attacks on Kuwait, demanding that the prisoners be freed. In 1984 terrorists hijacked a Kuwait Airways plane, killing two, and bomb explosions killed several innocent civilians in two seaside cafés. In 1985, a TWA flight was hijacked and an

In December 1983 a bulldozer clears rubble from the U.S. embassy in Kuwait, the target of the first terrorist attack in the country's history.

assassination attempt was made against Kuwait's emir. In 1988 another Kuwaiti civilian airliner was hijacked.

These terrorist activities in Kuwait prompted a tough government crackdown. Sheik Jabir investigated, arrested, and prosecuted the terrorists as criminals. Kuwait's government also passed a tough antiterrorism bill and expelled thousands of foreigners suspected of supporting terrorist goals. With these tough government responses, Kuwait set an example among Middle Eastern countries for effectively fighting terrorism. To suppress future Islamic violence, Jabir also took actions that affected much of Kuwait's population. He imposed restrictions on constitutional freedoms such as freedom of the press and assembly, gave state security police broader powers, and increased restrictions and surveillance of the Shia community, where many were suspected of having connections with Iranian Shia Islamists. As Cordesman notes, "The Kuwaiti government . . . allowed the political police, internal security forces, and royal intelligence to investigate and arrest individual [Shias] without adequate cause."[25] These actions upset many Kuwaitis who were concerned about civil freedoms and caused many of Kuwait's Shia who did not support the Iranians to feel that they were being unfairly persecuted and excluded from Kuwait's government.

Following the initial rash of terrorism, most Islamic fundamentalists in Kuwait have confined their activities to political involvement in the country's National Assembly. There, various Islamist groups, composed of both radical fundamentalist Muslims and more moderate individuals, and both Sunnis and Shias, joined with merchants and liberals to oppose the policies of the emir and ruling family and to argue for an expansion of democracy in Kuwait. This Prodemocracy Movement has battled the ruling family for years, rallying each time the emir suspended the National Assembly. The Islamists in Kuwait, however, have shown they will break from their prodemocracy allies when it comes to social and religious issues. In 1999, for example, the Islamists joined forces with tribal members of the Assembly to block a decree that would have given Kuwaiti women the right to vote, even though it was supported by their liberal opposition colleagues.

In the most recent elections in Kuwait, in July 2003, the Islamists won more seats in the National Assembly than ever before, twenty-three out of fifty. However, many of the most radical Islamists were not reelected. As reporter Adel Darwish explains, "While overall the Islamists scored impressive successes in the voting, most are Salafis [one branch of fundamentalist Muslims] who tend to confine their activities and aspirations to the Arabian peninsula. The Islamists suspected of having links with radical groups lost most of their seats."[26] What effect the Islamists might have on Kuwait in the future is not yet known.

5

SOCIETY AND LIFESTYLE

In many ways Kuwaiti society is in transition, caught between its traditional past and the recent effects of its oil wealth. Oil has allowed Kuwaitis to enjoy a modern, free, and affluent lifestyle saturated with Western influences. On the other hand, by opening the door to new values and attracting foreigners to the country, oil has also helped to create many divisions, both religious and cultural, in Kuwaiti society. These tensions have become part of life in contemporary Kuwait.

KUWAITI ETHNIC GROUPS AND DIVISIONS

The population of Kuwait, according to CIA 2003 estimates, is mostly Arab—about 45 percent native Kuwaiti Arabs and about 35 percent Arabs from other areas. The remaining 20 percent is made up of South Asians (9 percent), Iranians (4 percent), and miscellaneous other ethnic groups. Arabic is the official language, but English is widely spoken.

The main social division in Kuwait is between Sunni and Shia Muslims. The ruling family, many high-ranking members of the government, and many prominent Kuwaitis are members of the majority Sunni sect of Islam. Although some Shia Muslims have been appointed to the Cabinet and other high-level government posts, Shias tend to be underrepresented in Kuwait's government and social elite. In addition, particularly in the crackdown following the terrorist activity in the 1980s, Shias have faced discriminatory treatment from the government. This has caused some Shias to resent the government and the power of the Sunnis within Kuwaiti society, increasing tensions between the two groups.

Although most Kuwaiti citizens are relatively well off because of generous government benefits, income and class divisions do exist. The wealthiest Kuwaitis are members of the ruling al-Sabah family, descendants of the original Bani Utub tribe that first settled Kuwait. The next wealthiest are other Bani Utub descendants, members of Kuwait's influential class of Sunni merchants and traders. A small number of Shia families are also among the country's wealthy elite, but most Shias are not rich.

Other divisions in Kuwait's society stem from the country's efforts to define its citizenship narrowly. Exclusion of some population groups, such as longtime Bedouin residents and foreign workers, from citizenship and its many benefits has created a number of difficult social problems for Kuwait.

FROM BEDOUIN TO BIDOON

One group clamoring for Kuwaiti citizenship claims to be descended from Kuwait's early desert tribes, the Bedouin. After the discovery of oil, which allowed the Kuwaiti government to provide jobs and benefits to Kuwaitis, fewer and fewer tents were seen in the desert because Bedouin tribesmen moved to the cities to take advantage of government-sponsored education and job opportunities. For many years, Kuwait accepted these resettled tribal people and provided them with housing, free education and health benefits, and access to government

A woman in traditional dress watches a jet skier in Kuwait Bay. In Kuwaiti society, Western influences exist side by side with traditional Islamic practices.

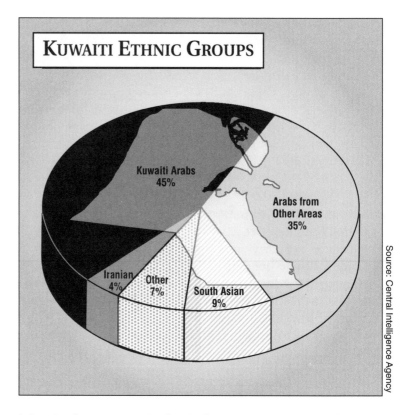

KUWAITI ETHNIC GROUPS

Kuwaiti Arabs
45%

Arabs from
Other Areas
35%

Iranian
4%

Other
7%

South Asian
9%

Source: Central Intelligence Agency

jobs. In fact, many Bedouin became citizens, and many worked in Kuwait's army and police force.

Bedouin peoples, however, were not limited to the boundaries of Kuwait. Most Bedouin were members of tribes that traveled throughout the region, sometimes into Kuwait but also into neighboring countries such as Saudi Arabia and Syria. The government came to believe that many, if not most, Bedouin residing in Kuwait were really people from other countries who were attracted to Kuwait because of its generous government benefits. In 1985, therefore, the Kuwaiti government adopted a new policy toward all Bedouin who could not prove long-term residency in Kuwait: It omitted them from the national census and classified them as noncitizens. Since most lacked citizenship to any other country, this group of stateless Kuwaiti residents became known as the Bidoon, which in Arabic means "without."

This government decision stripped the Bidoon of their rights to subsidized housing, health care, education, and other social benefits provided to Kuwaiti citizens; for example, Bidoon are now required to pay fees to utilize health care centers, while these services are free for Kuwaiti citizens. Next, in 1986, the government restricted Bidoon eligibility for travel documents; it also fired those without passports from government jobs (except the army or police) and instructed private employers to do the same. In 1987 and 1988 the government imposed more restrictions: It began refusing to issue Bidoon driver's licenses, expelling Bidoon children from schools and universities, and instructing Kuwaiti clubs and associations to dismiss their Bidoon members.

Conditions worsened for the Bidoon after the 1990 Iraq invasion of Kuwait. Their loyalty to Kuwait was questioned, and more than one hundred thousand fled the country or were expelled. After the war, those who had fled were not allowed to return to Kuwait, creating great hardship, separating families, and disrupting lives. Troubles also increased for Bidoon who remained in Kuwait; in 1993, the government decreed that they could no longer serve in Kuwait's military, where many Bidoon had been employed for years. Bidoon also found themselves increasingly facing government deportations. In 1999 and 2000, the government pressured the Bidoon to admit foreign nationality and renounce claims to Kuwait nationality in exchange for the opportunity to apply for a five-year residency permit; those who refuse are now subject to prosecution and deportation.

Today, an estimated 113,000 Bidoon reside in Kuwait. Many claim they have lived in Kuwait for generations, but because they cannot prove it, they are treated as illegal residents. The plight of the Bidoon remains one of Kuwait's most vexing social problems.

FOREIGN WORKERS/RESIDENTS

Another group excluded from Kuwaiti citizenship and benefits are its foreign workers. Many have lived in Kuwait for decades, bringing their families with them and bearing more children while in Kuwait. Indeed, according to 1985 census, as many as 30 percent of foreigners in Kuwait had been born in the country. Today foreigners make up 61.4 percent of the population.

Many Kuwaiti citizens fear that the foreigners will not want to leave and will demand citizenship for themselves. As a result of these fears, the Kuwaiti government has placed numerous

TRADITIONAL KUWAITI FOOD

Traditional Bedouin dishes, called *tabeekh*, are complete meals cooked in a single large pot over charcoal. Chicken, lamb, or fish are browned first, then mixed with vegetables and spices. Next, rice or wheat and water are added and the pot is left to simmer slowly. Kuwaitis still cook a number of traditional dishes at home in this manner. Indian and Persian influences are reflected in a more complicated method known as *marag*. Like tabeekh, the marag meal is cooked in a large pot, but the ingredients are first fried or boiled separately and then steamed together for the final presentation. Fish and meat marags are very popular in Kuwait.

These Kuwaiti dishes are heavily seasoned with Middle Eastern spices such as cardamom, cinnamon, cloves, coriander, cumin, ginger, nutmeg, black pepper, and paprika. They may be accompanied by common Middle Eastern staples such as *fuul* (a paste made from fava beans, garlic, lemon, and oil), *falafel* (deep-fried balls of chickpea paste with spices), and *houmos* (cooked chickpeas ground into a paste and mixed with garlic and lemon). In addition, Arabic flatbread, called *aish* ("life"), is eaten with everything. Islamic rules forbid alcohol and pork products.

A group of Kuwaitis shares traditional Bedouin dishes with American soldiers during the Gulf War.

economic, social, and political restrictions on foreigners. Non-Kuwaitis, for example, are not entitled to health care, education, and social benefits. They are prevented from holding certain jobs reserved for citizens, cannot earn wages as high as those available to Kuwaitis, and cannot form their own unions.

They also are prohibited from owning land or businesses, are not allowed to participate in Kuwait's stock market, and are subject to special taxes and fees. Socially, non-Kuwaitis are separated from Kuwaitis; they can live only in areas zoned for foreigners, and are segregated from Kuwaitis in sports and cultural activities. In addition, foreigners must earn a minimum amount in wages ($1,400 to $2,000 per month) before they are permitted to bring their families to Kuwait.

Political limitations against foreigners include strict laws that control the number of foreign workers admitted into Kuwait and laws that make citizenship difficult for them. Indeed, until 1980, only fifty foreigners were granted citizenship each year, and they had to meet certain rules—reside in Kuwait for a long period of time, be a Muslim, know Arabic, and contribute to the state. In 1980 the government loosened the requirements for citizenship, but not enough to drastically increase citizenship opportunities.

The unequal legal status between Kuwaitis and foreign laborers has produced a sharp division between the two groups within Kuwaiti society. Citizens often view foreign workers with hostility, and foreigners feel alienated and resentful about the discrimination directed against them. This alienation contributed to some foreign workers' siding with the invading Iraqi forces in 1991 and led the Kuwaiti government after the war to deport hundreds of thousands of foreign workers, particularly Palestinians, Iraqis, and Jordanians, whose leaders had not supported Kuwait during the war.

Today, Kuwait still has a need for large numbers of foreign workers, but it increasingly is turning to Asian nations such as India, South Korea, and the Philippines for these workers. As Crystal explains, "The government favors Asians because of their lower labor costs, and, because they are unable to speak Arabic or lay a claim to oil revenues on the basis of Arab nationalism, Asian workers are more apt to return home in a few years, thus raising fewer social and political issues."[27]

EDUCATION, HEALTH, AND WELFARE

Those who do hold Kuwaiti citizenship enjoy an amazing array of privileges and benefits, made possible by oil revenues. Education became the first priority after the discovery of oil; as early as the 1950s, the government began a massive education project to build schools and provide quality education, enabling Kuwait to develop one of the best school systems in the region. It included kindergarten and primary, middle, and secondary levels, and a law made education compulsory until the age of fourteen. In 1966, Kuwait University was established. Today, public education, from kindergarten through university, is provided free to Kuwaiti citizens; the government also will pay tuition and cover other costs to allow Kuwaitis to study abroad. These efforts have given Kuwait one of the highest literacy rates in the Middle East; in 2003, the country's literate population (defined as those at least fifteen years old who can read and write) was estimated at 83.5 percent.

Health care was the next area to be developed. Kuwait was the first Gulf state to offer free health care to its entire population, and though noncitizens' entitlement has since been restricted, over the years this investment resulted in dramatic improvements in public health. Infant and child death rates dropped significantly, and life expectancy for Kuwaitis increased by ten years to nearly seventy-seven years, about the same as in other industrialized nations.

Numerous other social services were added. The government spent large sums to create low- or no-cost housing developments and to provide Kuwaitis with low-interest housing

A young Kuwaiti does homework in 1952. Following the discovery of oil in the 1950s, improving education became a priority of the Kuwaiti government.

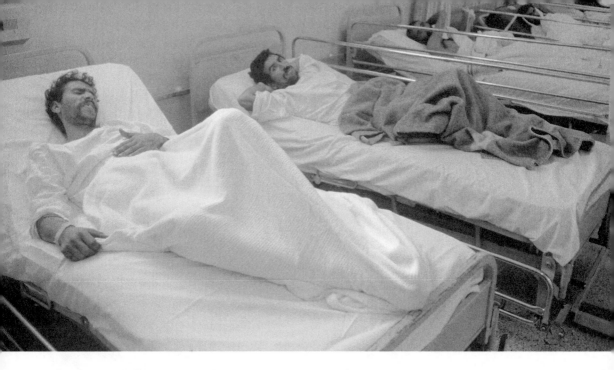

loans. In addition, it hired anyone needing a job, creating a large government bureaucracy that today employs the majority of working Kuwaitis. The government also developed pension programs for the elderly; aid for the disabled, low-income families, and others; and subsidies to lower the cost of food, transportation, gasoline, and utilities such as water, electricity, and telephone service. Other benefits include marriage payments—$13,000 given to couples when they marry, plus a $230,000 no-interest loan to buy or build a house.

The services and benefits available to Kuwaiti citizens are far beyond those provided in the United States or any other country. As Crystal puts it, "The range of privileges available to Kuwaitis is, by U.S. standards, awesome."[28] For all of these benefits, Kuwaitis pay no taxes.

Kuwaiti citizens like these men in a Kuwait City hospital receive free health care. As a result, Kuwait's life expectancy matches that of many other industrialized nations.

COMMUNICATIONS AND TRANSPORTATION

Thanks to oil riches, Kuwait has been able to invest lavishly in its infrastructure, providing its population with modern transportation and telecommunications systems. Kuwait's transportation system includes a total of 2,765 miles of well-maintained roads, 81 percent of which are paved. Expressways have been built in the coastal areas, connecting Kuwait City with other cities to the north and the south, and roads extend into Saudi Arabia and Iraq, uniting Kuwait with neighboring countries. A small bus service is available, but in such a small country, people travel largely by car. Therefore,

In 1991 a wealthy family celebrates Kuwait's liberation in their convertible. Most Kuwaitis have relatively expensive automobiles.

despite the extensive network of roads, traffic often becomes congested, with frequent traffic jams.

Kuwait has one international airport, located just south of Kuwait City. Kuwait Airways is the national airline, providing regularly scheduled flights to cities around the world. The country also has several large seaports. Two commercial ports, in Shuaiba and Shuwaikh, are among the largest and busiest in the Middle East, while ports at Mira Ahmadi, Mina Abdullah, and Mina Az-Zoor handle most of Kuwait's oil exports.

The country's communications system is also quite advanced. More than four hundred thousand telephone lines are in use, and the country has numerous pay telephones, providing excellent service. High-tech cable and satellite systems link Kuwait with its neighbors and much of the rest of the developed world, and a cellular telephone system operates throughout the country. Kuwait's telecommunications and transportation networks, severely damaged during the Gulf War, have been restored and improved.

Kuwaitis have satellite and local television reception and numerous radio stations, although these systems are under government control. Kuwait also has unrestricted Internet access, in both homes and cybercafés, as well as several independently owned daily newspapers that publish in both Arabic and English. Since formal press censorship ended in 1992, the press is free to debate most public issues, although a few subjects, such as the emir, are considered off-limits for criticism.

LIFESTYLE: AFFLUENCE AND TRADITION

Not surprisingly, considering the country's oil wealth and cradle-to-grave benefits, Kuwait's citizens today enjoy an affluent lifestyle. Kuwait has one of the highest per capita incomes in the world, estimated at $17,691.99 per person in 2003, and about 5 percent of the citizenry are millionaires.

Most Kuwaitis, like these men standing outside a Starbucks in Kuwait City, enjoy an affluent lifestyle.

Most Kuwaitis work for the government, either in government ministries or in industries such as oil, social services, transport, communications, energy, tourism, and defense. Kuwaiti stores sell the latest and widest variety of consumer goods and technology. Kuwaitis drive expensive, air-conditioned cars, talk on cell phones, shop at modern shopping malls, drink coffee at Starbucks, eat out at restaurants, and surf the Internet. Many live in big houses staffed by foreign servants. In almost every material way, Kuwaitis' lives compare to life in America.

However, these material riches and the resulting lifestyle improvements exist side by side with influences from Kuwait's past—the Islam religion and Arabic traditions and customs. Therefore, much of Kuwaitis' identity still revolves around religion, tradition, and especially family. The typical Kuwaiti eats most meals at home, surrounded by family, and evenings are also usually spent at home. Socializing often consists of large gatherings of extended family and friends, and men still socialize in the traditional *diwaniyas* just as their ancestors did, while women tend to congregate in their houses. Traditional coffee shops known *maqahas* are as popular as chain coffee shops, and traditional markets, or *souks*, have yet to be replaced by the new shopping malls. For recreation many Kuwaitis often return to the desert to go camping.

FOOD AND DRESS

The same mix of old and new is seen in other aspects of Kuwaiti life, such as food and dress. Both traditional Middle Eastern and a variety of foreign foods are available, and both Western and traditional clothing is worn.

Women in Kuwait wear everything from jeans to traditional clothes. Although many less conservative and more affluent Kuwaiti women dress in Western clothes, they are likely to choose more modest styles, in keeping with conservative Kuwaiti values. They also often cover their Western clothing when in public with a traditional Kuwaiti *aba*, a head-to-toe black cloak. Others, including more conservative Bedouin women, may also wear a traditional burka, a short black veil that covers the entire face, while some Muslim women wear the *hijab*, a headscarf that covers the hair but not the face.

Most Kuwaiti men, regardless of class, wear traditional clothing—usually a floor-length white or cream-colored robe

SOUKS: TRADITIONAL KUWAITI MARKETS

Although Kuwait has numerous modern supermarkets and shopping malls, many of its traditional markets (called *souks*) are still flourishing. In central Kuwait City, for example, there is a central city souk made up of about twenty different interconnecting markets. Each souk specializes in particular goods, such as clothing, hardware, or spices. This area is an interesting and cheap alternative to modern stores, but it requires shoppers to bargain for the best price. Tradional souks survive in other locations in Kuwait as well, such as Fahaheel and Jahra.

In addition, Kuwaitis shop at traditional open-air Friday markets (called souk al-juma'a) that sell everything from furniture and clothes to carpets, antiques, and livestock. Kuwait also has souks specializing in fresh food items such as meat, fish, fruits, and vegetables. The fish souks offer a variety of fish and crustaceans, much of it from the Arabian Gulf, and meat souks often feature fresh mutton and chicken. Small bakeries also can be found in Kuwait, preparing fresh breads on the spot. Prices at these markets are usually cheaper than at the large supermarkets, and foods are often much fresher. Finally, Kuwait is famous for its gold souks, which buy and sell gold jewelry, a very popular item among Kuwaitis. Kuwaiti gold jewelry is of unusually high quality, often 21 or 22 karat and exhibiting great workmanship. Pure gold bars can also be purchased.

called the *dishdasha*, along with leather sandals and an Arab headdress, which is made of a large piece of cloth that is folded into a triangle and then placed on the head with the ends hanging over the shoulders. This headgear provides shade in the summer, can be wrapped across the face during sandstorms, and can be twisted up into a turban while the wearer is doing manual work. In summer the headdress is usually white, changing to a red and white checked fabric in winter.

A wide variety of both foreign and traditional foods is available in Kuwait, due in part to the many foreigners living and working there. As one Web site puts it, "Kuwait is a food lover's paradise."[29] Gourmet and ethnic restaurants abound, serving European, Lebanese, Indian, Chinese, Japanese, Indian, Arabic, Thai, Italian, Iranian, and Moroccan dishes. Also available is traditional Kuwaiti food, which reflects a mix of Bedouin, Persian, Indian, and Eastern Mediterranean influences, including liberal use of pungent spices such as *baharat*, a common mix made of several Middle Eastern spices.

ARTS AND ARCHITECTURE

The Kuwait Towers in Kuwait City, the country's best-known landmark, combine traditional Islamic architecture with modern designs.

Kuwaiti arts and architecture celebrate both the nation's past and its present; new art forms exist side by side with traditional art. Modern Kuwaiti artists have exhibited their work both locally and abroad, promoted by the Society for Formative Arts. Theater is also celebrated in Kuwait; drama troupes from Kuwait have won numerous prizes and awards

all over the world. At the same time, the government actively preserves the country's traditional arts and crafts.

One of the most important traditional Kuwaiti art forms is a traditional Bedouin weaving process known as *al sadu*, a term that refers to a Bedouin loom. Bedouin women used the process to make the tents in which they lived, as well as utilitarian items such as rugs, cushions, men's coats, and saddlebags. Today, these crafts are displayed at the Sadu House, a museum in Kuwait City. Kuwait also has sought to preserve the folk art traditions of storytelling, poetry, folk dancing, and music, which often embody themes of the desert and the sea. Folk dancing, for example, is performed by men on special family and social occasions. One common dance is the *ardah*, a slow, graceful dance performed by groups of men gently swinging swords to the sound of drums, tambourines, and recitation of poetry. To keep its traditions alive, Kuwait in 1956 formed the Folklore Preservation Center, which collects, records, and classifies Kuwaiti folklore.

Islamic art is also common in Kuwait. Because Islam restricts artistic expression that realistically depicts humans or nature, this artwork typically features bold geometric or abstract designs. The National Museum in Kuwait City once displayed one of the world's most important collections of Islamic art. Unfortunately, the Iraqis looted and destroyed most of the museum's contents, as well as the museum itself, during the 1990 invasion. Today only a private collection of Islamic art survives, at the nearby Tareq Rajab Museum.

Like its art, Kuwait's architecture is both traditional and modern. Traditional Kuwaiti homes were simple structures made of local materials such as mud and palm leaves and adorned with paintings, mosaic patterns, and Islamic ornamentation. A typical house had a central courtyard with a series of rooms built around it, as well as a separate area or building called the *diwaniya* (or parlor), where the men would gather, entertain other men, smoke, enjoy snacks, and discuss politics. A few of these old homes have been carefully preserved by the government.

As oil began flowing, Kuwait began commissioning modern architecture of glass, steel, and concrete, designed by the world's foremost architects. Perhaps the country's best-known landmark is the Kuwait Towers, located in Kuwait City. The gigantic and striking set of three towers can be seen

THE ANCIENT KUWAITI SPORT OF FALCONRY

Falconry, a sport that involves deploying birds of prey for hunting, originated in Kuwait's desert culture, where it was originally a useful method of supplementing with game the meager desert diet of dates, milk, and bread. Indeed, falcons have long been admired among Arabs for their beauty, loyalty, keen eyesight, and excellent hunting abilities, and they quickly became an important part of Arab heritage. Today, falconry is a popular sport in Kuwait. Two main species of falcon are used, saker and peregrine falcons. Wild falcons are trapped and trained for the hunting season, which starts in November. While soaring high in the sky, falcons can spot any movement of their prey more than a mile away. Once in pursuit of prey, the falcon flies very fast, makes a sudden dive at tremendous speed, and grabs its prey with its sharp claws and beak. Trained falcons then bring the prey back to their handlers. Traditionally, falcon hunting parties will clean their game and cook it over an open fire while boasting about the skill and courage of their falcons.

The sport of falconry originated in Kuwait's desert culture and remains popular today.

from most parts of Kuwait City and has become a symbol of modern Kuwait. The towers rise to form globes that house observation decks, rotating restaurants, and water reservoirs. Another impressive modern building is the huge, elaborately decorated Grand Mosque. Made of concrete and stone, it has a main prayer court that can accommodate ten thousand men at prayer time, and its interior surfaces are covered with Islamic designs and calligraphy. Government buildings also showcase modern designs. The National Assembly building, for example, is a cement structure shaped like a Bedouin tent.

SPORTS AND LEISURE

As in any affluent country, leisure activities abound in Kuwait. It should not be surprising, given Kuwait's close relationship with the sea, that Kuwaitis spend a lot of time near the waters of the Gulf. During the hot months, the cooling breezes from the sea invite walks along the shoreline as well as indulgence in every type of water sport, including swimming, sailing, yachting, motorboating, waterskiing, raft racing, wind surfing, scuba diving, and fishing.

In addition, Kuwait has developed a thirteen-mile waterfront project in the capital; it features five man-made public beach areas as well as extensive landscaping that has created lush, shady areas for various leisure activities. One part of the project is a yacht club covering twenty-nine acres. It has a marina big enough for 265 craft and is surrounded by man-made protective wave breakers. Another area is Green Island, a 39.5-acre man-made island connected to the mainland. It showcases numerous plants, shrubs, and trees and offers a lagoon for swimming and water games, restaurants, a children's play area, and a large, open-air amphitheater used for concerts. Other attractions along the waterfront include a large water park, a swimming pool complex with Olympic-size pools; tourist resorts, and an ice-skating rink.

Kuwaitis' favorite sport is soccer (called football in Kuwait). Kuwaitis also enjoy such sports as car racing, tennis, basketball, and golf. For native Kuwaitis and visitors wealthy enough to afford the country's luxuries, Kuwait offers beauty, diversity, and much stimulation.

6

KUWAITIS LOOK TO THE FUTURE

With its abundant oil reserves and strategic Middle East location, Kuwait will continue to hold a secure position in world affairs as long as industrialized countries such as the United States are dependent on oil. Threats from Iraq diminished with the overthrow of Saddam Hussein by a U.S.-led military coalition in 2003. Kuwait now can focus its resources and attention on its three main long-term challenges: strengthening its economy, stabilizing its political system and society, and developing its defenses and foreign relations.

ECONOMIC REFORMS

One of Kuwait's most important long-term goals is planning for a future in which its oil is depleted—a process that will undoubtedly take a long time. Fortunately, the country still has large reserves of oil that will last many years; as Clements notes, "Kuwait has [enough] proven oil reserves . . . [to last] at current production levels for one hundred and fifty years."[30]

Nevertheless, since the early days of the oil industry, Kuwait's economic planners have prepared for the day oil eventually runs out by using some of Kuwait's oil earnings to make substantial investments in foreign countries. In the 1950s and 1960s, for example, Kuwait began making investments in properties and businesses in Britain and the United States. In 1976 the government established the Reserve Fund for Future Generations, an investment fund designed to support future generations of Kuwaitis once oil resources are depleted. It placed about $7 billion into the fund at the outset and mandated that 10 percent of its oil revenues be invested in the fund each year. These investments have been enormously successful. Indeed, by 1990 the country was earning more from its foreign investments than from its oil exports. As of late 2003, the fund was worth around $65 billion.

Oil prices are expected to remain strong because of increasing world demand; as Nawaf S. al-Sabah, manager of Kuwait Petroleum Corporation USA, explains, "As [Kuwaitis] look into the future, we recognize that the global oil demand will be increasing and that much of this demand will be on Gulf crude from Kuwait, Saudi Arabia, and the United Arab Emirates. . . ."[31] The Kuwaiti government's strategy, therefore, is to boost oil production in its rich northern fields with the help of international oil firms that have the technology and expertise to do the development work.

Increased production, however, may cause Kuwait's oil to be depleted sooner. Experts inside and outside the country therefore agree it is crucial for Kuwait to diversify its economy to develop industries other than oil. As Abdul Mohsin Yousef al-Hunaif, an undersecretary in Kuwait's Finance Ministry, has stated, "Over-reliance on oil is a major issue. We do not control prices, quantity and currency. It is dangerous to just depend on oil."[32] The government hopes to start this process by diversifying the oil industry to create income sources other than just the sale of crude oil, by increasing Kuwait's refining

Kuwaiti oil is transported across the country through pipelines like these. In recent years, the government has taken steps to develop industries other than oil.

capacities and moving into related industries such as petro-chemicals. Kuwaiti officials, however, know that other types of industry must also be encouraged.

To this end, the Kuwaiti government plans to transfer many government-owned industries to private ownership, which, it is hoped, will improve profitability and productiv-ity through competition. The government has already sold most of its shares in investment companies, banks, and fi-nancial institutions, and it hopes to do the same for telecom-munications, power and water, and other sectors of the economy. Other important economic reforms cited by ex-perts as critical for Kuwait include encouraging foreign in-vestments and reducing the huge government spending on social programs.

So far, Kuwait has made very slow progress in these areas. A privatization law, which would allow private companies to buy major public utilities, has yet to be approved by the National

Firefighters lower a valve into place to cap a Kuwaiti oil well sabotaged in the Gulf War. Iraqi soldiers sabotaged hundreds of oil wells during the war.

Kuwaiti stockbrokers enjoy a break on the trading floor. In 2000 the government opened Kuwait's stock exchange to foreign investors.

Assembly, and a five-year economic plan proposed by the government in 1999 to reduce government employment and subsidies did not succeed. In 2000, however, one reform was implemented: The National Assembly passed a foreign investment bill eliminating the requirement that foreign companies have a Kuwaiti sponsor or partner and allowing foreigners to own companies listed on Kuwait's stock exchange. With this law, Kuwait hopes to attract more foreign investment, which should help broaden its private-sector economy.

Experts say measures to restructure Kuwait's economy are needed not only to diversify the economy but also to reduce Kuwait's reliance on foreign skilled and technical labor while Kuwaiti citizens (93 percent) fill high-paid, unproductive government jobs. This imbalance has caused social problems, created a huge, unnecessary government bureaucracy, and produced a native workforce with poor work habits and an unwillingness to take difficult, manual, or low-paying jobs.

The solution, Cordesman argues, is to "create an economy that offers its citizens real job opportunities and reduces its dependence on foreign labor."[33] The keys to this change, Cordesman and other experts say, are extensive privatization (to create high-paying jobs in the private sector that will attract native Kuwaitis), better education (to train Kuwaitis for

HUMAN RIGHTS IN KUWAIT

According to the U.S. Department of State, despite commendable democratic practices, Kuwait still is guilty of human rights abuses. After the liberation of Kuwait in 1991, for example, thousands of non-Kuwaitis were arbitrarily detained or arrested on suspicion of collaborating with the Iraqi invaders. There were many reports of government beatings and torture to extract confessions from suspected collaborators; indeed, as many as fifty Palestinians and other foreigners were tortured to death by police or military personnel. More recent human rights concerns include prison overcrowding and the abuse of detainees during interrogation by some police and members of security forces, such as the Criminal Investigation Division (CID) and Kuwait State Security (KSS). In addition, U.S. officials claim that the Kuwaiti judiciary is subject to influence from other branches of government and that a pattern of bias exists against foreign residents. Critics also argue that the government infringes on citizens' privacy rights; for example, security forces sometimes monitor activities and communications, and the government sometimes restricts freedom of speech, the press, assembly, and association. Other problems identified by the U.S. government include some limits on freedom of religion, violence and discrimination against female domestic servants of foreign origin, and a failure to protect the job rights of Bidoon and foreign workers.

employment in the private sector), budget cuts (to reserve government welfare benefits for poor citizens), and greater participation by educated Kuwaiti women, which would expand the available native workforce.

SOCIAL AND CITIZENSHIP REFORMS

In addition to the foreign laborer problem, Kuwait's society may be threatened in the future by the country's denial of citizenship to certain groups. A major goal of the prodemocracy movement, therefore, has been to increase citizenship rolls to allow more people in Kuwait to vote and participate in government. Currently, because of the limits on citizenship, only about 10 to 15 percent of Kuwaitis, or roughly one hundred thousand out of a population of almost a million, are eligible to vote in the National Assembly elections.

Efforts to make these voting reforms have met, so far, with limited success. In 1999 an attempt was made in the National Assembly to pass legislation to give women the vote, but it was narrowly defeated by the Islamists and traditional Bedouins, or tribalists, who opposed the idea of women's being involved in politics. Following their loss in the Assembly, women activists in Kuwait filed court cases arguing that the election laws prohibiting them from voting were unconstitutional. Kuwaiti courts rejected these claims, ending their hopes of gaining political rights through the court system. On May 16, 2004, however, Kuwait's cabinet approved a draft law allowing women's voting; the draft still needs the approval of the Assembly to become law.

Efforts to solve the problem of the Bidoon have not fully succeeded either. In 2000, the National Assembly passed legislation that required all Bidoon to register with the government and allowed a small number of Bidoon to apply for citizenship. The law provides for up to two thousand Bidoon each year to be granted citizenship, but only if they can prove substantial connections with Kuwait. Examples of these connections include serving with Kuwaiti troops during the 1967 and 1973 Arab-Israeli wars, registering in the 1965 census, DNA proof that they have Kuwaiti ancestors, or proof that they are the wives, children, or relatives of Kuwaiti citizens. The U.S. State Department has called the new application process slow and ineffective. In 2000, only 1,647 Bidoon were granted citizenship; since then, thousands more have become citizens, and the government has begun providing some services to the Bidoon. Unless Kuwait takes bolder action to resolve this issue, however, many Bidoon will simply never be able to meet the difficult requirements for citizenship, leaving a significant portion of the Kuwaiti population stateless and insecure. Such a large group of disgruntled people, many of them young, deprived of basic rights such as education and jobs, could seriously endanger Kuwait's security and its future.

DEFENSE AND FOREIGN RELATIONS

Economic and social reforms must be linked with Kuwait's defense and security needs. As Cordesman notes, "the same geography that has blessed Kuwait with oil has cursed it with neighbors like Iran and Iraq."[34] Although Iraq's aggressive regime appears to have been eliminated, Iraq remains a highly insecure and destabilized country. Kuwait and other Gulf nations are concerned that the violence and terrorism

POLITICAL GROUPS IN KUWAIT

Although political parties are illegal in Kuwait, several political groups have formed and have begun to assume functions similar to those of political parties. The major political groups in Kuwait include:

The Islamic Constitutional Movement (ICM)—a Sunni fundamentalist religious group

The Islamic Popular Grouping—also a Sunni fundamentalist religious group

The Islamic National Alliance—the main group of Shia Muslims

The Kuwait Democratic Forum (KDF)—a loose association of nonreligious (secular) groups

The National Democratic Group—an organization of generally secular progressives with liberal tendencies

Tribal confederations or grouping— hold primaries, and agree to vote for certain candidates to protect tribal interests

The Independents—identified as those with no other specific classification and who tend to be aligned at various times with either the ruling family or the other political groups

These groups have become more and more active in recent years, giving a greater voice to various parts of Kuwait's society and reflecting religious and tribal values as well as more liberal views.

in Iraq could spread throughout the region. Until a stable, clearly friendly government is established in Iraq, Kuwait's leaders must continue to consider Iraq a potential threat. In addition, Kuwait's central Middle East location, long and easily penetrable desert borders, and limited military continue to make it vulnerable to other outside forces that may covet its oil riches. Finally, because of its limited water and agricultural capacity, Kuwait will always be dependent on imports of food and water, creating another military vulnerability.

To meet these threats, military experts believe that Kuwait needs modern weapons and strong defense forces capable of rapid deployment. Kuwait has already begun this process of modernization. Following the Iraqi invasion, it increased spending on weapons and military preparedness, and by 1994–1995, Kuwait's total military spending had reached $5.4 billion. This translates into about $1,907 per year for each Kuwaiti citizen, more than the United States' per capita defense spending. These expenditures have improved Kuwait's military forces, giving it a greater ability to respond to threats and low-level attacks from countries such as Iran and Iraq.

Perhaps the biggest challenge facing Kuwait in its plans to upgrade its defenses is a lack of manpower. Its small population provides only a limited number of males of military age to draw from for its armed forces—about 102,000 males between the ages of 13 and 17, about 78,400 between the ages of 18 and 22, and 140,800 between the ages of 23 and 32. Furthermore, Kuwait has no mandatory draft and has reduced its existing armed forces by eliminating as many as 10,000 Bidoons and failing to enlist many Kuwaitis who fought against the Iraqis.

It will likely take many years for Kuwait to acquire all the new weapons it has ordered and staff a larger and more

Kuwaiti soldiers learn to assemble grenades during the Gulf War. The war underscored the weakness of Kuwait's military forces.

KUWAIT'S VULNERABLE BORDERS

Kuwait has historically been vulnerable to military strikes and invasions because of its long desert borders—it shares a 155-mile border with Saudi Arabia and a 149-mile border with Iraq. Kuwait's border with Iraq has been a particular source of tension for Kuwaitis. This border was established by Britain in 1923, and Iraq accepted it in its 1932 application to the League of Nations for membership as an independent state. However, Iraq later asserted a claim to rule Kuwait and refused to recognize the country's independence in 1961. Finally, in 1963, Iraq signed a treaty with Kuwait recognizing its independence and borders. Yet border disputes between the two countries continued over the decades, culminating in the 1990 Iraqi invasion of Kuwait. Following Kuwait's liberation, a United Nations commission formally set the Iraqi-Kuwaiti border, basing it on the 1963 treaty, and Iraq has since recognized this as the true border.

Today, despite the lessened threat from Iraq, Kuwaitis remain conscious of the vulnerability of their borders. Kuwait's terrain consists largely of flat desert plains with few defensive barriers, and numerous roads link it with neighboring countries. Armored forces therefore can easily move into Kuwait, requiring the country to maintain high military vigilance.

capable military force. Once men and equipment are assembled, Kuwait still faces the challenge of training its military to enable it to defend an attack on Kuwait's borders. It also will remain dependent on foreign technical assistance to help operate its new weapons systems until Kuwaitis can take over these functions. Meeting these challenges will be critical to improving Kuwait's security.

Yet most agree that Kuwait's forces will never be strong enough on their own to defend its vulnerable geographic position. Experts say, therefore, that Kuwait must also focus on foreign policy and diplomacy, reinforcing its ties with other Gulf nations and continuing its close relationship with the United States. Kuwait is already a member of the Gulf Cooperation Council, a coalition of Persian Gulf nations (including Kuwait, Saudi Arabia, Bahrain, Qatar, Oman, and the United Arab Emirates) established in 1981 to strengthen cooperation in agriculture, industry, investment, security, and trade. However, the Council has been criticized for failing to make progress in the area of collective defense. In the future,

Kuwait hopes its Gulf partners can coordinate and integrate their military defenses, weapons spending, and training to develop an effective collective defense system capable of responding to and repelling outside military threats against any member of the group.

For the foreseeable future, Kuwait looks to the United States for military protection. In April 2001, Kuwait and the United States renewed their 1991 defense pact, allowing U.S. forces to use Kuwaiti facilities and station troops and equipment in Kuwait for another ten years. Kuwait's close relationship with the United States, however, also presents problems and risks for Kuwait. Many Kuwaitis fear that their country will become too dependent on the United States and will fail to develop its own and regional defense capabilities. Others express concerns about growing Western influences in Kuwait and possible Islamic terrorist attacks on Kuwait due to its friendship with America. Indeed, Kuwait experienced one such attack in January 2003, when terrorists linked to the anti-American terrorist group al Qaeda attacked U.S. Marines on Failaka Island. Kuwait's challenge, therefore, is a familiar one—to keep its foreign alliances strong enough to guarantee protection, but not so strong that they begin to erode Kuwait's independence or threaten its society.

POLITICAL LIBERALIZATION

Disputes between the emir and the Assembly have so far largely prevented the two sides from working together to address Kuwait's economic, social, and defense challenges. Instead, Kuwaiti politics have been marked by the continuing struggle between those seeking greater democracy and the more authoritarian impulses of the ruling family and government. This struggle has been reflected in demands by the Assembly for more power and greater legislative control over the emir. Middle East analyst Peter L. Cooper predicts that "until the executive and legislative branches of government figure out how to overcome their differences, Kuwaiti politics will remain paralyzed."[35]

Some recent changes, however, bode well for those seeking to curb the power of the royal family and promote greater democracy. Although political parties are still illegal, political groups and associations in Kuwait have become much more prominent and active in government since the Gulf

Many Kuwaitis believe that the new prime minister Sheik Sabah (pictured with Colin Powell in 2004) will introduce a number of beneficial economic reforms.

War. In addition, in July 2003 the emir decreed that the office of prime minister, traditionally filled by the crown prince, would be opened to other members of the royal family and potentially to nonroyals. This reform was a key demand of the prodemocracy opposition because it allows the prime minister more independence and opens the door for the appointment of other exceptionally well-qualified individuals. For now, the prime minister is Sheik Sabah al-Ahmad al-Sabah, Kuwait's former foreign secretary. Finally, most posts in the new cabinet were awarded to people who are not members of the ruling family, another sign of political liberalization.

Many in Kuwait hope that the new government, headed by Prime Minister Sheik Sabah, will be able to bridge the differences between the ruling family and the Assembly. Unlike the previous prime minister, who was ill and often disengaged from politics, Sheik Sabah is respected for his competency and is said to favor privatization and other economic reforms. His appointment is viewed as a good sign that Kuwait may soon embrace deeper economic restructuring.

On the other hand, the July 2003 elections brought a new crop of members into the National Assembly, changing the makeup of the legislature in ways that could hinder the government's modernization plans. The elections dramatically increased the number of Islamists and decreased the number of liberals in the Assembly. This diminished the role of more secular groups who tend to support more Western ideas of Kuwait's future. Instead of promoting unity between Kuwait's government and its Assembly, therefore, this development sets the stage for increased political conflict.

The Islamist Movement

The 2003 Assembly elections confirmed that a large part of the current political struggle in Kuwait involves the degree to which the country will be ruled by Islamic law and culture, and the degree of Western influence that will be permitted. Islamists and tribalists oppose Western influences and want to see Kuwait return to the values of its past and the Islamic religion. They have introduced legislation seeking to reinforce conservative and religious values—for example, requiring Kuwaiti women to wear traditional clothing, including the veil, and banning concerts in Kuwait. As Islamist Assembly member Waleed Tabtabai has explained, "Islamic parties oppose the Western behaviour in this community, like the women voting and the Western concert music that we see. . . . Also we oppose the new Western clothes that have invaded this country and the hairstyles and also the tradition we see

A member of the Islamist movement holds up the Koran during a 2004 protest against American involvement in the Middle East. Islamists wish to rid Kuwait of all Western influence.

among the youth of smoking and drinking liquor."[36] This conservative attitude is very attractive to many Kuwaitis.

Others in Kuwait see the strict Islamist interpretations of Islam as restrictive and incompatible with building a modern and free Kuwait. In the past, Islamists along with their conservative tribal allies have opposed modernizing programs offered by the emir, many of which were supported by liberal groups. Islamists were successful, for example, in blocking the women's vote, which they opposed because they want women to continue in their traditional roles. Some Islamists also have opposed economic reforms such as privatization and foreign investment in Kuwait's oil sector, because they do not want foreign, particularly Western, companies involved in Kuwait's economy. In addition, Kuwait's Islamists have warned of the dangers of U.S. troops in Arab countries, a development they fear may lead to a loss of Arab independence.

The newly elected Islamists, however, are by no means uniform in their views. Indeed, many are seen as moderate and likely to support the vote for women, economic reforms, and a continued alliance with the United States. As reporter

Holding a poster of Jabir al-Ahmad al-Sabah, Kuwaiti women celebrate the emir's return after the Gulf War. Choosing a successor for the emir is Kuwait's most pressing political issue.

Amir Taheri states, "It is thus hard to sustain the claim that the new parliament represents a setback for Kuwaiti democracy. On the contrary, it may prove to be more supportive of a free-enterprise economy, more socially tolerant and even more pro-West."[37]

How this issue of the Islamization of Kuwait ultimately is resolved will have a major effect on the country's future. If Islamists control or dominate the legislature in the future, they may be able to impose greater religious restrictions on Kuwait society and block parts of the agenda for economic and political reforms being pushed by the government and other groups. On the other hand, coalitions may form between moderate Islamists and other groups to prevent drastic social changes and to allow many reform measures to pass.

QUESTIONS OF SUCCESSION

Instability in the legislature is coupled with uncertainty about who will succeed the emir, Sheik Jabir al-Ahmad al-Sabah, who is in his seventies and almost completely incapacitated by health problems. Sheik Saad al-Sabah, the crown prince, is next in line to lead Kuwait, but he too is elderly and in ill health. The emir's decision in 2003 to appoint Sheik Sabah to the position of prime minister helped provide needed daily leadership to the country, but he suffers from heart disease, and the fourth in line, Sheik Salim al-Sabah, is unable to succeed because he suffers from Parkinson's disease.

Long-term political stability will depend upon the ruling family's agreeing on a ruler and the Assembly's responding positively to that choice. Although there may be some confusion while the al-Sabah family tries to come to agreement about future leadership, observers of Kuwait's political scene say that complete chaos is unlikely given the country's long history of stable al-Sabah leadership. The more likely scenario, given the uncertainties both in the Assembly and within the ruling family, is continued government ineffectiveness for the next several years.

Kuwait's future is intricately linked with resolution of its political issues. If political unity can be achieved, the country's many blessings—an educated population, a century's worth of oil reserves, a booming economy, and the United States as its defender—promise Kuwait a bright future and a prominent role in the Middle East.

FACTS ABOUT KUWAIT

GEOGRAPHY

Location: Middle East, bordering the Persian Gulf between Iraq and
 Saudi Arabia

Area: 6,880 square miles (water: 0 square miles; land: 6,880 square miles)

Area comparative: slightly smaller than New Jersey

Bordering countries: Iraq and Saudi Arabia

Coastline: 309 miles

Climate: dry desert; intensely hot summers; short, cool winters

Terrain: flat to slightly undulating desert plain

Natural resources: petroleum, fish, shrimp, natural gas

Land use: arable land, 0.34 percent; permanent crops, 0.06 percent;
 other, 99.6 percent

Natural hazards: sudden cloudbursts, common from October to April,
 bringing heavy rain that can damage roads and houses; sandstorms and dust storms, occurring throughout the year but most
 common between March and August

Environmental issues: limited natural freshwater resources (some of
 world's largest and most sophisticated desalination facilities provide much of the water); air and water pollution; desertification

PEOPLE

2004 estimates:

Population: 2,257,549 including 1,291,354 nonnationals

Age and gender: 0–14 years, 27.5 percent (male, 316,237; female,
 304,671); 15–64 years, 69.8 percent (male, 1,007,298; female,
 569,128); 65 years and over, 2.7 percent (male, 38,408; female,
 21,807)

Population growth rate: 3.36 percent

Birth rate: 21.85/1,000 population

Death rate: 2.44/1,000 population

Infant mortality rate: 10.26 deaths/1,000 live births

Life expectancy: 76.84 years (male, 75.86 years; female, 77.86 years)

Fertility rate: 3.03 children born/woman

Ethnic groups:

Kuwaiti: 45 percent

Other Arab: 35 percent

South Asian: 9 percent

Iranian: 4 percent

Other: 7 percent

Religions:

Muslim: 85 percent (Sunni, 70 percent; Shia, 30 percent)

Christian, Hindu, Parsi, and others: 15 percent

Languages: Arabic (official); English widely spoken

Literacy (age 15 and over):

Total population: 83.5 percent

Male: 85.1 percent

Female: 81.7 percent

GOVERNMENT

Name: State of Kuwait, or Kuwait

Government type: Nominal constitutional monarchy

Capital: Kuwait (Unofficially called Kuwait City)

Administrative divisions: Five governorates—Al Ahmadi, Al Farwaniyah, Al'Asimah, Al Jahra', Hawalli

National holiday: National Day, February 25

Independence: June 19, 1961 (from Great Britain)

Constitution: Approved and enacted November 11, 1962

Legal system: Civil law, with Islamic law significant in personal matters

Suffrage: Adult males who have been naturalized for 30 years or more or have resided in Kuwait since before 1920, and their male descendants at age 21

Executive branch:

Chief of state: Amir Jabir al-Ahmad al-Jabir al-Sabah (since December 31, 1977)

Prime Minister: Sabah al-Ahmad al-Jabir al-Sabah (since July 13, 2003)

Cabinet: Council of Ministers appointed by the prime minister and approved by the monarch (Note: The monarch is hereditary, not elected; prime minister and deputy prime ministers are appointed by the monarch.)

Legislative branch:

Unicameral National Assembly or Majlis al-Umma (50 seats; members elected by popular vote to four-year terms); elections last held July 6, 2003, resulting in 21 seats for Islamists, 14 for government supporters, 3 for liberals, and 12 for independents

Judicial branch: High Court of Appeal

Political parties and leaders: None; formation of parties is illegal

Flag: Three equal horizontal bands of (from top) green, white, and red, with a black trapezoid based on the hoist side

ECONOMY

Labor force: 1.3 million (about 80 percent non-Kuwaiti) (1998 estimate)

Industries: petroleum, petrochemicals, desalination, food processing, construction materials

Agricultural products: Practically no crops; fish
Exports: $22.29 billion
Imports: $9.6 billion
Debt: $11.2 billion
Economic aid: $0
Currency: Kuwaiti dinar (KD)

NOTES

INTRODUCTION: TRANSFORMED BY OIL

1. Anh Nga Longva, *Walls Built on Sand: Migration, Exclusion, and Society in Kuwait.* Boulder, CO: Westview, 1997, p. 28.

CHAPTER 1: DESERT BY THE SEA

2. Jill Crystal. *Kuwait: The Transformation of an Oil State.* Boulder, CO: Westview, 1992, p. 2.

3. Longva, *Walls Built on Sand,* p. 19.

4. Frank A. Clements, *Kuwait.* Santa Barbara, CA: Clio, 1985, p. ix.

CHAPTER 2: HISTORY OF A "LITTLE FORT"

5. H.V.F. Winstone and Zahra Freeth, *Kuwait: Prospect and Reality.* New York: Crane, Russak, 1972, p. 53.

6. Winstone and Freeth, *Kuwait: Prospect and Reality,* p. 53.

7. Longva, *Walls Built on Sand,* p. 20.

8. Quoted in Miriam Joyce, *Kuwait, 1945–1996: An Anglo-American Perspective.* Portland, OR: Frank Cass, 1998, p. xii.

9. Winstone and Freeth, *Kuwait:* Prospect and Reality, p. 80.

10. Crystal, *Kuwait: The Transformation of an Oil State,* p. 12.

11. Crystal, *Kuwait: The Transformation of an Oil State,* p. 16.

12. Simon C. Smith, *Kuwait, 1950–1965: Britain, the al-Sabah, and Oil.* New York: Oxford University Press, 1999, p. 137.

13. Joyce, *Kuwait, 1945–1996,* p. 3.

CHAPTER 3: INDEPENDENT KUWAIT

14. Jill Crystal, "Kuwait," *Persian Gulf States: Country Studies,* Helen Chapin Metz, ed. Washington, DC: Government Printing Office, 1994, p. 82.

15. Joyce, *Kuwait, 1945–1996,* p. 166.

16. Joyce, *Kuwait, 1945–1996,* p. 167.

17. Quoted in Crystal, *Kuwait: The Transformation of an Oil State,* p. 160.

18. Quoted in Crystal, *Kuwait: The Transformation of an Oil State,* p. 161.

19. Anthony H. Cordesman, *Kuwait: Recovery and Security After the Gulf War.* Boulder, CO: Westview, 1997, p. 64.

20. Quoted in Ashok Dutta, "Picking Up the Pace: The Removal of Saddam Hussein's Regime Has Produced Significant Responses in Neighbouring Kuwait." *MEED Middle East Economic Digest,* October 10, 2003.

CHAPTER 4: RELIGION, TRADITION, AND CULTURE

21. William Smyth, "Historical Setting," *Persian Gulf States,* p. 38.

22. Quoted in Kuwaitiah, "The Religion of Kuwait." www.kuwaitiah. net/religion1.html.

23. Helen Rizzo, Katherine Meyer, and Yousef Ali, "Women's Political Rights: Islam, Status and Networks in Kuwait." *Sociology,* August 2002.

24. Rizzo, Meyer, and Ali, "Women's Political Rights."

25. Cordesman, *Kuwait: Recovery and Security,* p. 60.

26. Adel Darwish, "Kuwait: Kuwait Goes to the Polls: The Kuwaiti Elections Threw Up Some Interesting Candidates and a Host of Political Conundrums." *The Middle East,* August/September 2003.

CHAPTER 5: SOCIETY AND LIFESTYLE

27. Crystal, "Kuwait," *Persian Gulf States,* p. 52.

28. Crystal, *Kuwait: The Transformation of an Oil State,* p. 70.

29. Kuwait Information Office, "Cuisine," www.kuwait-info.com/ sidepages/culture_cuisine.asp.

CHAPTER 6: KUWAITIS LOOK TO THE FUTURE

30. Clements, *Kuwait,* p. xiii.

31. Quoted in Joanne Chan and Margaret Vernon, "Going Global: The Future of Kuwaiti Oil." *Georgetown Journal of International Affairs,* Spring 2004, www.pwcglobal. com/extweb/NewCoWeb.nsf/0/ 03F 69B8ED68ECB5185256E5300493D 92?OpenDocument.

32. Quoted in "New Momentum, New Hope: Kuwait's Economy Will Grow Rapidly This Year After a Decade of Disappointment, But Major Reform Is Needed if the Pace Is to Be Maintained." *Middle East Economic Digest,* October 10, 2003.

33. Cordesman, *Kuwait: Recovery and Security,* p. 51.

33. Cordesman, *Kuwait: Recovery and Security,* p. 58.

35. Peter J. Cooper, "Challenges for Kuwait's Policymakers," May 3, 2004. AME Info FZ LLC, www.ameinfo.com/news/Detailed/38838. html.

36. Quoted in Frank Gardner, "Kuwait's Crossroads." BBC News, January 15, 2001, http://news.bbc.co.uk/1/hi/world/middle_east/1118036.stm.

37. Amir Taheri, "Ku-waiting for Reform." New York Post, July 11, 2003, www.benadorassociates.com/article/459.

CHRONOLOGY

325 B.C.
Bedouin tribes roam the Arabian deserts, and an ancient civilization lives on Failaka Island off the coast of Kuwait.

A.D. 571–632
The prophet Muhammad is born and founds the religion of Islam in the Middle East. After his death in A.D. 632 Islam is spread throughout the region and into Kuwait.

1534
Arabia becomes part of the Ottoman Empire.

1710
A small fishing settlement called Kuwait is founded by the Bani Utub people.

1752
The al-Sabah family emerges as political leaders in Kuwait.

1775
Sheik Abdallah I begins a relationship with Britain to help ward off attacks by the Wahhabis, a group of zealous fundamentalist Muslims.

1818
The Ottomans defeat the Wahhabis after Kuwait forms closer relations with the Ottoman Empire.

1896
Sheik Mubarak I (Mubarak the Great) seizes power by killing his brothers, Muhammad and Jarrah, who were closely aligned with the Ottomans.

1899
Britain and Kuwait sign a formal treaty under which Britain promises to protect Kuwait from foreign attackers and Kuwait pledges loyalty to Britain.

1920
Wahhabi forces attack Kuwaiti troops in the Battle of Jahrah;
Britain sends air and sea support that allows Kuwait to win.

1923
Saudi Arabia places an embargo on Kuwaiti goods, a policy
that disrupts Kuwait's trading.

1930
Japan's development of cultured pearls destroys Kuwait's
pearl industry.

1934
Sheik Ahmad al Jabir al-Sabah signs an agreement giving oil
drilling rights to Kuwait Oil Company (KOC), a jointly
owned British-American company.

1938
KOC discovers massive oil reserves in Burgan oil field,
south of Kuwait Bay. Kuwaiti merchants organize to demand reforms in the way Kuwait is governed—a struggle
later called the Majlis Movement.

1946
Kuwait begins to develop its oil industry after World War II ends.

1950 February 25:
Sheik Abdallah Salim takes the throne and uses Kuwait's
new oil revenues to implement an ambitious development
plan that seeks to turn Kuwait into a modern power. The effort requires Kuwait to import many foreign workers.

1961 June 19:
Kuwait declares independence from Britain. Britain and
Kuwait negotiate letters of friendship that provide for
Britain to give up control over Kuwait, although it contin-
ues to provide military support.

Iraqi premier Abdul Karim Qassem announces that all of
Kuwait is a part of Iraq. Britain sends troops to protect Kuwait.

Kuwait is admitted to the Arab League.

1962
A provisional government established by Sheik Abdallah drafts
Kuwait's first constitution. It is approved on November 11.

1976

The National Assembly's criticism of the ruling emir, Sabah Salim, causes him to dissolve the Assembly and suspend parts of Kuwait's constitution guaranteeing freedom of assembly and free speech.

1981–1984

During the Iran-Iraq War, Iranian forces bomb Kuwaiti oil installations and attack Kuwaiti ships in the Gulf, threatening the country's oil trade. The United States places eleven Kuwaiti tankers under U.S. registry and protection, beginning a strong U.S.-Kuwaiti relationship.

1982

Kuwait's stock market crashes.

1983

Islamic terrorists bomb U.S. and other Western embassies and facilities in Kuwait. Later terrorists hijack Kuwaiti planes, murder an Iraqi diplomat, and unsuccessfully attack the emir.

1985

The Kuwaiti government adopts a new policy toward Bedouin, classifying as noncitizens all those who cannot show documentation of long-term residency in Kuwait.

1986

Sheik Jabir suspends the National Assembly after it criticizes members of the ruling family for their handling of the 1982 Kuwaiti stock market crash. Afterward, Assembly members, merchants, and others organize the Prodemocracy or Constitutional Movement, calling for the Assembly to be reinstated and for constitutional reforms.

1990 August 2:

Kuwait is invaded and occupied by Iraqi forces, beginning the Persian Gulf War.

October:

The emir meets with the prodemocracy opposition and agrees, when the war is over, to restore Kuwait's original 1962 constitution and reconstitute the National Assembly.

1991 January 16:
A UN military operation led by the United States, called Operation Desert Storm, is launched to force Iraq to leave Kuwait.

February 26:
UN forces liberate Kuwait. Kuwait begins reconstruction from the damages of war.

September:
Kuwait signs a ten-year joint defense agreement with the United States.

1992
Elections are held for a new National Assembly.

1994
The National Assembly passes a law extending citizenship to the sons of naturalized citizens.

1999
The emir dissolves the National Assembly a third time and immediately holds new elections. The new Assembly votes down a bill that would have given Kuwaiti women the right to vote.

2000
The Kuwait National Assembly passes legislation that allows some Bidoon to apply for citizenship. Another piece of legislation is a foreign investment bill changing Kuwaiti law to allow foreigners to own 100 percent of companies listed on Kuwait's stock exchange.

2001
Kuwait and the United States renew their defense agreement for another ten years.

2003
The United States topples the regime of Saddam Hussein in Iraq, reducing the historical Iraqi military threat and helping to spur an economic boom in Kuwait. In July elections, Islamists win the largest block of seats ever in the National Assembly. Also, the emir decrees that the office of prime minister will be opened to qualified individuals other than the crown prince.

FOR FURTHER READING

BOOKS

Fred Bratman, *War in the Persian Gulf.* Brookfield, CT: Millbrook, 1991. A discussion of the Persian Gulf crisis, from the Iraqi invasion of Kuwait in 1990 to Iraq's defeat in 1991.

Leila Merrell Foster, *Kuwait.* New York: Childrens Press, 1998. Explores Kuwait's history, geography, economy, language, religion, sports, arts, and people.

Leila Merrell Foster, *The Story of the Persian Gulf War.* New York: Childrens Press, 1991. Examines the causes and events of the Persian Gulf War that followed Iraq's invasion of Kuwait in 1990.

Geography Department, *Kuwait in Pictures.* Minneapolis, MN: Lerner, 1989. Provides numerous colorful photographs and text introducing the geography, history, government, people, culture, and economy of Kuwait.

Solomon A. Isiorho, *Modern World Nations: Kuwait.* Philadelphia: Chelsea House, 2002. An overview of Kuwait, its history, geography, economy, government, and society.

WEB SITES

Kuwait Information Office (www.kuwait-info.org). A Web site run by the Kuwait Information Office, an organization established by Kuwait's Ministry of Information to foster an understanding of Kuwait's politics, society, culture, economy, and security needs by the U.S. political, media, academic, and business communities.

Bureau of Consular Affairs, U.S. Department of State (http://travel.state.gov). A U.S. government Web site providing information for people who plan to visit Kuwait.

Arab Net (www.arab.net). A site run by a Saudi Arabia news service providing online resources on the Arab world, primarily dealing with countries in the Middle East and North Africa.

CIA: The World Factbook (www.cia.gov). A U.S. government Web site for the CIA, providing geographical, political, economic and other information on Kuwait.

WORKS CONSULTED

BOOKS

Frank A. Clements, *Kuwait.* Santa Barbara, CA: Clio, 1985. A comprehensive bibliography with an informative introduction.

Anthony H. Cordesman, *Kuwait: Recovery and Security After the Gulf War.* Boulder, CO: Westview, 1997. An exploration of the impact of the Gulf War on Kuwait and a discussion of the challenges facing the country in the future.

Jill Crystal, *Kuwait: The Transformation of an Oil State.* Boulder, CO: Westview, 1992. A well-known and often-cited profile of Kuwait that discusses its history and the economic, social, and political tensions and transformations caused by oil discoveries.

Jill Crystal, *Oil and Politics in the Gulf: Rulers and Merchants in Kuwait and Qatar.* New York: Cambridge University Press, 1990. An exploration of the effect of oil on Kuwait's politics, economy, and society.

T.M. Hawley, *Against the Fires of Hell.* New York: Harcourt Brace Jovanovich, 1992. A detailed study of the environmental effects of the Gulf War in Kuwait.

Miriam Joyce, *Kuwait, 1945–1996: An Anglo-American Perspective.* Portland, OR: Frank Cass, 1998. A history of Kuwait from the end of World War II to the late 1990s, covering the period of Kuwait's transformation from a small sheikdom to a modern oil-producing state.

Anh Nga Longva, *Walls Built on Sand: Migration, Exclusion, and Society in Kuwait.* Boulder, CO: Westview, 1997. A study of Kuwait's society throughout its history, with a focus on the way foreign workers have affected the country.

Helen Chapin Metz, ed., *Persian Gulf States: Country Studies.* Washington, DC: Government Printing Office, 1994. An overview of the geography, history, economy, society, and politics of Kuwait.

Haya al-Mughni, *Women in Kuwait: The Politics of Gender.* London: Saqi, 2001. A study of women activism in Kuwait, including the contemporary effort to win the right for women to vote.

Simon C. Smith, *Kuwait, 1950–1965: Britain, the al-Sabah, and Oil.* New York: Oxford University Press, 1999. A history of the relationship between Kuwait and Britain, beginning with the country's post–World War II expansion of its oil industry to just after its 1961 independence.

H.V.F. Winstone and Zahra Freeth, *Kuwait: Prospect and Reality.* New York: Crane, Russak, 1972. A general history of Kuwait, from its inception through 1971.

PERIODICALS

APS Diplomat, "Redrawing the Islamic Map: Kuwait—The Question of Succession," August 19, 2002.

Adel Darwish, "Kuwait: Kuwait Goes to the Polls: The Kuwaiti Elections Threw Up Some Interesting Candidates and a Host of Political Conundrums," *The Middle East*, August/September 2003.

Ashok Dutta, "Picking Up the Pace: The Removal of Saddam Hussain's Regime Has Produced Significant Responses in Neighbouring Kuwait," *MEED Middle East Economic Digest*, October 10, 2003.

Helen Rizzo, Katherine Meyer, and Yousef Ali, "Women's Political Rights: Islam, Status and Networks in Kuwait," *Sociology*, August 2002.

INTERNET SOURCES

BBC News, "1991: Jubilation Follows Gulf War Ceasefire," February 28, 1991. http://news.bbc.co.uk/onthisday/hi/dates/stories/february/28/newsid_2515000/2515289.stm.

Bureau of Democracy, Human Rights, and Labor, U.S. Department of State, "Kuwait: Country Reports on Human Rights Practices," March 31, 2002. www.state.gov/g/drl/ rls/hrrpt/2002/18280.htm.

Center for Research Studies on Kuwait, "Failaka Island," 2003. www.crsk.org/failaka1.htm.

Joanne Chan and Margaret Vernon, "Going Global: The Future of Kuwaiti Oil," *Georgetown Journal of International Affairs*, Spring 2004. www.pwcglobal.com/extweb/NewCoWeb.nsf/0/03F69B8ED68ECB5185256E5300493D 92?OpenDocument.

CNN, "Marines in Fatal Assault Had No Amino," October 9, 2002. www.cnn.com/2002/WORLD/meast/10/08/kuwait.marines.shot.

Energy Information Administration, U.S. Department of Energy, "Kuwait Country Analysis Brief," March 2003. www.eia.doe.gov/emeu/cabs/kuwait.html.

Global Security, "Failaka Island," October 10, 2002. www.globalsecurity.org/military/facility/failaka.htm.

Haitham Haddadin, Reuters, "Young Kuwaitis Revive Lost Craft of Pearl Diving," September 2, 2003. www.kuwait-info.org/News/pearl_diving.html.

Human Rights Watch, "Kuwait: Promises Betrayed—Denial of Rights of Bidun, Women, and Freedom of Expression," October 2000. http://hrw.org/doc/?t=mideast&c=kuwait.

Kuwait Information Office in India, "The Constitution." www.kuwaitinfo.com/sidepages/state_constitution.asp.

Kuwait Information Office in India, "Cuisine." www.kuwaitinfo.com/sidepages/culture_cuisine.asp.

Kuwait Information Office in India, "Kuwait Overview." www.kuwaitinfo.com/sidepages/nat_over.asp.

Kuwait Information Office in India, "Liberation." www. kuwait-info. com/sidepages/gulfwar_liberation.asp.

Kuwait Information Office in India, "Shopping." www. kuwait-info. com/sidepages/tourism_shoppingguide.asp.

Kuwait Information Office USA, "Falconry—An Ancient Art," 2002. www. kuwaitinfo.org/Country_Profile/society_and_culture/addl_links/society_and_culture_addl_links_falconry.html.

Kuwait Information Office USA, "Geography," 2002. www. kuwait-info. org/For_Students/kuwait_geography. html.

Kuwait Information Office USA, "Kuwaiti Women," 2002. www.kuwait-info.org/women.html.

Kuwait Information Office USA, "The Political System in Kuwait: An Overview," 2002. www.kuwait-info.org/Fact_Sheets/political_system.htm.

Kuwaitiah Net, "The Religion of Kuwait." www.kuwaitiah.net/religion1.html.

Lonely Planet, "Kuwait," 2003. www.lonelyplanet.com/destinations/middle_east/kuwait/printable.htm.

Permanent Mission of the State of Kuwait to the United Nations, "Al-Sabah Rulers of Kuwait," 2004. www.kuwaitmission.com/rulers.htm.

Daniel Pipes, "Kuwait's Terrorism Policy Sets an Example, *Wall Street Journal*, November 18, 1986. www.danielpipes. org/ zarticle/173.

Reuters, "Kuwait Approves Draft Law Giving Women the Vote," May 17, 2004. www.jihadwatch.org/dhimmiwatch/archives/2004/05/001980print.html.

Amir Taheri, "Dimming the Kuwait City Lights: Kuwaitis Return to Their Tribal Roots," *National Review Online,* July 17, 2003. www.benador associates.com/article/477.

Amir Taheri, "Ku-waiting for Reform," *New York Post*, July 11, 2003. www.benadorassociates.com/article/459.

UPI, "Terrorists Launch Second Attack on U.S. Marines in Kuwait," News-Max.com Wires, October 10, 2002. www. newsmax.com/archives/articles/2002/10/9/172035.shtml.

World Statesmen, "Kuwait Chronology." www.worldstatesmen.org/Kuwait.htm.

Yahoo, "Kuwait Culture," 2002. http://sg.travel.yahoo.com/guide/middle_east/kuwait/culture.html.

Yahoo Travel, "Kuwait," 2003. http://sg.travel.yahoo.com/guide/middle_east/kuwait/index.html.

INDEX

Picture Credits

About the Author

Debra A. Miller is a writer and lawyer with an interest in current events and history. She began her law career in Washington, D.C., where she worked on legislative, policy, and legal matters in government, public interest, and private law firm positions. She now lives with her husband in Encinitas, California. She has written and edited publications for legal publishers as well as numerous books and anthologies on historical and political topics.